REVOLUTIONARY
CHESTERTOWN

REVOLUTIONARY
CHESTERTOWN

LOYALISTS & REBELS ON MARYLAND'S EASTERN SHORE

THEODORE CORBETT

FOREWORD BY KAREN EMERSON

Charleston · London

THE
History
PRESS

Published by The History Press
Charleston, SC 29403
www.historypress.net

Unless otherwise noted, all photographs are by the author.

First published 2014

Manufactured in the United States

ISBN 978.1.62619.399.4

Library of Congress CIP data applied for.

*Dedicated to the Kent County Historical Society, which has done
so much to make this book possible.*

Contents

Foreword

Chestertown, Maryland, played an important part in the history of the American Revolution, and Ted Corbett realized this. He came to the Kent County Historical Society and made friends immediately. Not only had he lived in the same part of New York where I was from, but he had also written five books on history and wanted to write a sixth book on Chestertown during the American Revolution.

After spending hours researching in the society's library, he has produced a wonderful volume fully explaining the unique issues that involved this part of the Eastern Shore during the war. Mr. Corbett has captured the essence of an area that was an important port, the geographic center of the American colonies and the "breadbasket of the Revolution."

Chestertown remains much the same today as then; visitors are fortunate enough to be able to walk the brick sidewalks and see many of the same buildings discussed in the book. It is easy to picture Thomas Smyth in Widehall, and the replica of the *Sultana* at the dock at the foot of High Street makes you certain that you have just seen William Geddes. Mr. Corbett's in-depth look makes it all very clear.

KAREN EMERSON
Executive Director, Kent County Historical Society

Acknowledgements

In writing this book, I have been aided by a warm contingent of people in Kent County. I spent many weeks in the Kent County Historical Society Library, where librarian Joan Anderson and I carried on continuous and inspiring discussion. She read the entire manuscript and introduced me to her involvement in the Turner's Creek area. Along with Joan, the busy Karen Emerson also read the entire manuscript and was always encouraging. I also want to thank the organizers of the Chestertown Book Fair, which acquainted me with regional book people and allowed me to find my mapmaker, Catherine Escarpeta, who did a superb job. My brother Jim Corbett again acted as advisor.

Introduction

Back in the eighteenth century, Maryland's Eastern Shore was part of the British Empire. It was different in that its settlement was ethnically and religiously homogenous. Kent was its wealthiest county and, after 1730, Chestertown its largest town. We assume that this success bred tranquility, offering little impetus for the people to participate in the conflict of the Revolutionary era. Kent County produced no Maryland military heroes like William Smallwood and Mordecai Gist (although they did recruit there), and no battles were fought there. Its naval commanders had lackluster or abortive careers, and its rebel leaders rarely made a name for themselves in state government. With the Anglican Church vestries dominant, religious evangelism was opposed, so as to maintain the peace. What dangers existed were attributed to Loyalists, who were regarded by rebels as annoying vandals.

But this is misleading because Kent County and Chestertown were not tranquil. Throughout the war, a civil conflict took place on the Eastern Shore between rebels and Loyalists, in which Kent County played a role. It focused on the Loyalist bands preventing the recruitment of rebel militia and on the disruption of food supplies for the Continental army. Both were crucial to George Washington as he attempted to conduct war in the Middle Colonies. In addition, political conflict existed with the state government in Annapolis to the point that some regarded it as a greater enemy than the British Crown. The crux of the situation was in the new terms of the Maryland Constitution of 1776, which were not new at all in the sense that they perpetuated the rule of Western Shore grandees. The Eastern

Shore also had its grandees, who, in contrast to those of the Western Shore, favored an expansion of the franchise and a reduction of requirements to hold office. Many Eastern Shore grandees sought to avoid politics, although they continued to support the rebel cause. Another source of disruption was the Methodist factor, a rising alternative to the vestries' domination of the Anglican Church. The vestries insisted that the Methodists were Loyalists because they were evangelistic, refused to bear arms and opened their meetings to slaves.

Having highlighted the immediate reality of Kent County and Chestertown, we then focus on how these situations developed. The book begins with Kent County's planters, many of whom became grandees and developed the richest plantations and farms on the Eastern Shore. We then look at Chestertown, which attracted planters because of their interest in trading tobacco and wheat in the Atlantic world. They hoped to create another Annapolis, with mansions that were elegant centers of enterprise. Next, we investigate Kent County's three Anglican parishes, each featuring a ruling vestry established by the Maryland Assembly, which governed religious affairs through them. While parsons complained and rivalries existed within the parishes, the overall façade of the Anglican churches remained stable until the war, when a lack of parsons and the presence of Methodists became a challenge. We then look at the lesser elements of society, like modest farmers, who, rather than the grandees, were actually the backbone of Kent County's economy. We see how the middling sort established mills, granaries and handicraft production while remaining in the countryside rather than moving to Chestertown. The lesser sort served chiefly as field hands, but some became skilled in milling or brick-making enterprises and could be hired out by their masters. On account of the backbreaking work, they had short life spans.

The following chapters carry us fully into the war as political thought, courtesy of Philadelphia publishers, inspires Kent County's leaders through the works of John Dickinson, Thomas Paine and James Chalmers. We see that their ideas had much more in common than is usually expected. After considerable delay, some in Kent County joined the movement for independence, wrote Tea Resolves and sympathetically provided flour for the poor of the closed port of Boston. We then cross to Annapolis and back as Maryland's conventional government gives way to the Constitution of 1776, causing the debate over the franchise. Kent County's own Committee of Correspondence gives way to the state-controlled Committee of Observation.

This is followed by an analysis of what it takes to go to war, whether one served as volunteer, Minuteman, militiaman or Continental regular. The role of Kent County and Chestertown as the breadbasket of the Continental army is highlighted, as opposed to its lackluster militia. Kent County's Commissioners of Supply feared the Loyalists, and in at least one case, a commissioner found that they had burned his mills to the ground. Loyalism came in different degrees of conviction and covered every social element. At the end of the war, many Loyalists left Kent County and the Eastern Shore for Canada, notably those serving in the first battalion of Maryland Loyalists, commanded by James Chalmers.

THE EIGHTEENTH-CENTURY EASTERN SHORE

Chestertown and Kent County are part of a larger region, Maryland's Eastern Shore. The region's most significant geographical feature is Chesapeake Bay, a waterway and transportation corridor that splits Maryland in two. The Eastern Shore of Chesapeake Bay expands inland and along with Delaware and a portion of Virginia creates the Delmarva Peninsula. The peninsula, cut by rivers, creeks, inlets and bays, is mostly flat farmland where wheat, corn and tomatoes still grow and where poultry and cattle are raised. In the eighteenth century, it was a patchwork of tidal waterways and marshes, strewn with farmsteads, crossroads churches and a few ports. To serve the expansive farming area, ports were rarely located on the bay or even at the mouth of a river but rather as far upriver as navigable.

Plantations appeared, staples like wheat were grown and ports were designated to ship these to the British Isles and the West Indies. Yet middling and small farms were dominant in numbers, and wheat production was often supplemented by livestock, naval stores and lumber for a West Indies market. The plantations were rarely as large or slave labor as extensive as on the Western Shore of the bay. The economy depended on the ability to ship commodities from its local ports. An alternative Philadelphia connection by water and land developed in the second half of the eighteenth century and was reflected in the presence of Pennsylvania merchants and investors in Chestertown. Chestertown's merchants tried to ignore Western Shore Baltimore, but after the Revolution, that city took over Chesapeake Bay's trade, a shift from which the Eastern Shore's economy never recovered.

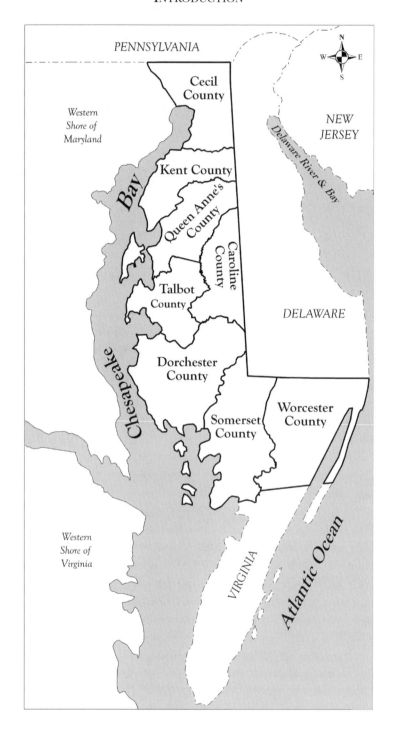

The Eastern Shore, circa 1775. *Drawing by Catherine Escarpeta.*

Counties were established as the chief local government on the shore. Their seventeenth-century boundaries were extensive, but gradually, they became more manageable as the Maryland legislature designated them between the important rivers or transportation corridors. Kent County, for instance, was reduced from its expansion boundaries of 1642 to roughly the area between the Sassafras River in the north and the Chester River in the south. Each county had a courthouse. At the time of the Revolution, eight counties had been established on the Eastern Shore; from north to south, they were Cecil, Kent, Queen Anne's, Caroline, Talbot, Dorchester, Somerset and Worcester.

Just before the Revolution, the Eastern Shore's population reached eighty-eight thousand, a substantial 46 percent of Maryland's population. It was larger than several colonies, including New Hampshire, Rhode Island, Delaware and Georgia. Thus, the region had more resources to contribute to the Revolutionary era than is realized.

Chapter 1

Kent County Planters

As the Eastern Shore evolved in the seventeenth century, 90 percent of the settlers came from England and the remaining 10 percent from Scotland and Ireland. Thus, by the eighteenth century, the region's population was made up of third- and fourth-generation families who had originally come from the British Isles. Ultimately, as ethnic homogeneity went hand in hand with religious uniformity, the established Anglican Church and its vestries monopolized most believers, especially the leading planters. At the top of society, these planters established great estates and then built Chestertown. Kent County would become an economy of enterprising and intermarried merchant-planters, diversified agriculture, tenanted middling whites and, most conspicuously, extensive slavery that made it part of the Chesapeake region. Originally, the planters were rough-hewn—neither poor nor wealthy. Some would succeed by the mid-eighteenth century in accumulating great wealth, resulting in deference to them and a mania for all things English. Such men were grandees and would provide a degree of leadership when the War for Independence came.

THE EARLY YEARS

In the seventeenth century, despite the steady immigration inspired by the toleration of religion and land policies of the Calvert family's Lord Baltimore,

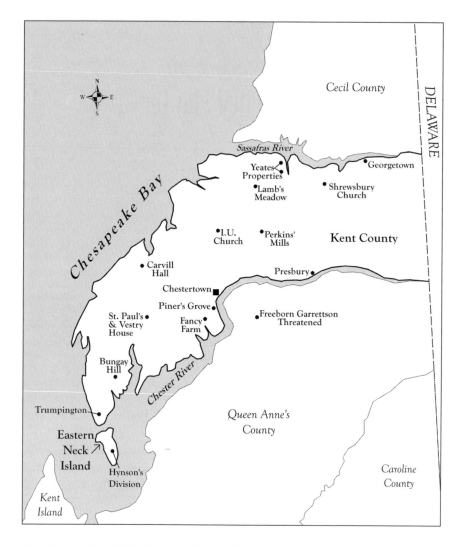

Kent County, circa 1780. *Drawing by Catherine Escarpeta.*

the Chesapeake region grew very slowly. The path of migration for settlers to Kent County was to move eastward from Kent Island across Kent Narrows and up the Chester River. By 1706, Kent County was much reduced and confined to its modern boundaries. In 1712, there were 2,886 inhabitants in the county. Most of the population had arrived before the early 1700s, and the majority of the residents had been born in Kent County. By the mid-eighteenth century, immigrants found their opportunities limited and merely passed through the Eastern Shore on their way to greener pastures. The population developed without them, perpetuating the dominance of already existing families.

A Seventeenth-Century Farming Community

Kent County became a market-oriented agricultural community in which planters measured their success by the accumulation of land and labor. To improve their lots, settlers took certain steps to achieve this goal. First, they formed households and rented land. They then purchased a plantation and eventually obtained the labor of servants and slaves. The poorest struggled to form a household and favored the security of being a tenant, but it was difficult to move up. A minority of white males could supplement their farming income as a carpenter, cooper, blacksmith or tanner. The purchase of land raised one's independence, status and ability to provide for his children. To be successful as a planter, one had to use capital to hire labor. After the 1680s, the market for servants declined, and the slave market rose. Servants had the disadvantage of being short-term laborers, fulfilling their indentures in four to seven years and then leaving. Masters abused their servants constantly, but the servants did have the right to take them to Kent County Court, where they seem to have gotten fair trials.

The Need for Slaves

Eastern Shore planters bought slaves in the West Indies or from New England merchants who were returning from Barbados. Eventually, Chestertown merchants and mariners also participated in the trade by going directly to the West Indies. Male slaves were more expensive than servants, but they lasted a lifetime. A gradual improvement in Atlantic trade connections lowered the cost of slaves. Still, a single slave was far too expensive for the average tenant to afford—but this could be offset in the overall picture by the planters buying more slaves. By 1755, slaves made up 25 percent of Kent County's population.

On the plantations and farms, male slaves outnumbered females because of the need for field hands and thus a native-born black population did not appear for several years. African slaves lived in small groups, and this helped to ensure the persistence of African cultural traditions. Life was tedious and physically demanding. From sunrise to sunset, they raised cash crops of tobacco and, later, wheat and tended livestock and vegetable gardens. They fished and worked as boatmen and performed menial tasks such as cooking, cleaning, sewing and washing. Some became skilled craftsmen or blacksmiths, and their owners found they could lease them profitably to other whites. Others resisted their bondage by refusing to work and running away.

STAPLE CROPS

In the seventeenth century, tobacco established its primacy as a profitable cash crop and became the main reason for acquiring land. To better handle the tobacco trade, the Maryland Assembly authorized the purchase of half-acre plots at convenient landing places along the rivers and creeks, to be called "Public Landings," "where tobacco may be brought in order to be waterborne and conveyed to any town of this province." Upon this land, the commissioners were authorized "to build rolling houses not to lie above two furlongs from the water." The tobacco, placed in casks, was rolled from the plantations to the landings.

In the following century, diversification of farming production became the norm in Kent County; now the planters would no longer be dependent on the fluctuating and vulnerable tobacco market. Wheat production offered advantages over that of tobacco, especially for the tenant farmer. While the ground had to be prepared for sowing both crops, once this was accomplished, the wheat no longer needed cultivation. Harvesting of wheat required only two or three weeks of hard labor, during which seasonal labor could be hired. After that, threshing by a treading horse was immediate, although this process could be postponed and the grain stored until prices were higher. The acreage planted in wheat was limited only by the cost of harvest labor, and if neighbors agreed to help each other with the brief harvest, the acreage in cultivation could be even more expansive. As the chief labor-saving crop, wheat was most profitable for Kent County's average tenant farmer as well as its great planters. The second most popular staple was Indian corn, which accompanied the wheat and thus created a grain trade.

Kent County led the rest of the Eastern Shore and, ultimately, all of Maryland away from the tobacco staple and into the production of wheat.

A view of contemporary Kent County showing a wheat field on the expansive landscape. Kent County led the Eastern Shore in the production of wheat by the 1750s and was a hub of the "breadbasket" during the Revolution.

By 1719, over a quarter of Kent County's value in crops was devoted to wheat. After the 1750s, while tobacco by no means disappeared from Eastern Shore fields, the percentage of its production and shipments fell drastically. As Chestertown's position in the tobacco trade declined, its position in the grain trade pulled even with the port of Oxford, and by 1769, it had surpassed Oxford and was challenging Annapolis and Baltimore. Planters increased their profits from grains not because of progressively better prices for the crop but because they were able to increase production without forcing the price down. However, the demand for wheat did fluctuate, making income unsteady.

THE TEXTURE OF THE COUNTRYSIDE

It was in the countryside that the economy was born and prospered, not in urban centers, which came much later. On creeks, gristmills rather than sawmills predominated, and brick granaries were the chief identification of a landing. Every planter had to be a merchant, especially before Chestertown and Georgetown existed, as evidenced by the crucial wharfs and docks at every plantation of any size.

The early Anglican church, St. Paul's, was an isolated one, where the faithful came from miles around and the vestry dominated weekly Sunday festivities. Like St. Paul's, those churches that came later stood alone in a place central to the parish. Likewise, Maryland courthouses were not always built in town but rather at a central rural crossroads, facilitating travel from all areas.

The Yeates house, built circa 1760, was part of the development of Turner's Creek by Donaldson Yeates and his nephew, John Lathim. The original plank building may have served as both a store and residence.

By the mid-eighteenth century, country stores began appearing at crossroads and along rivers and streams. While these stores may have been supplied by merchants from Chestertown or Georgetown, they served the local population independently and linked them to the broader consumer world. Most of them looked like houses rather than commercial establishments, as the retail merchant typically combined his shop with his living quarters. A good example is Donaldson Yeates's store, which was located at Turner's Creek close to where it enters the Sassafras River. The store, constructed in two parts, was probably erected in the 1760s, when Yeates purchased the property. The early freestanding structure was built of wood plank with chinking, a practice that, because few examples have survived, was more widespread than is thought. A brick addition was constructed in the 1780s when Yeates's business partner and nephew, John Lathim, took over the store.

RISING FAMILIES OF PLANTERS

In the seventeenth century, most immigrants coming to the Eastern Shore were single males. Because it was difficult to find a mate, the family alliances that later became so crucial were nonexistent. When immigration slackened and daughters of the first settlers reached marriageable age, the population became increasingly native born, the sex ratio evened and the number of children and average family size increased. The planter's wife preceded his sons in inheritance, and upon his death, the widow was charged with the task of prudently selecting a new husband. A parent primarily sought to provide a farm for each son, ignoring the rules of primogeniture. Thus, a majority of heads of households came to own land.

At first, these planters were unable to replicate English conditions in the forests of the Eastern Shore. They were often younger sons, without the support of families in England or Maryland. Only after making several voyages to the Chesapeake did they settle on the Eastern Shore. There, they were preoccupied with work, a need to succeed materially and a concern to provide adequately for each of their sons. They sought to re-create the trading situations between English ports like London rather than follow the ideal of retiring to the agrarian countryside. Planting alone was not sufficient for accumulation of wealth unless they could educate their sons to improve their farms or hire middling overseers. Caught up in crop cultivation and trade, planters had little time for gentility or leisure pursuits.

In fact, the emerging families did not get along with one another. In 1656, the Kent County Court witnessed an altercation between Thomas Ringgold and Joseph Wickes. Ringgold's infraction involved the slaughtering of a sow, which Wickes claimed he did not own. In turn, Ringgold sued Wickes for fathering an illegitimate child. Wickes retorted that "it was better [to] be a whore master than a thief as [Ringgold] was." This conflict between families showed that society considered the rights of property far more important than sexual promiscuity on the part of males.

THE NEW PROSPERITY

In the following century, peaking in the 1760s, native-born families became the basic economic and social unit. Their successful estates now covered between one thousand and twenty thousand acres. They consisted of two or more plantations, typically using forty slaves as field hands to annually plant and harvest tobacco, wheat and corn. However, the bulk of the estate's crops came from half a dozen smaller farms that were tenanted out or managed by their relatives or an overseer. Pasture, wood lots, fallow fields and mills made up the rest of the estate. Thus, to make an estate successful, planters had to deal with their broader family and tenants. Centers of enterprise were dispersed throughout an estate rather than coming from a single plantation.

In the mid-eighteenth century, the most prosperous planters or their sons also served as merchants or lawyers, allowing them to operate independently. Holding office also helped in making revenues available. As a landed gentleman, a planter could choose to stand for election to represent any county or district in which he held property. To be considered successful, a grandee had to hold plantations, be appointed to a government position, own and renovate a town house and attend horse races. Deference in elections was shown to this group by the lower orders of society and even by some of the upper orders.

By the 1760s, Chestertown's merchant-planters had extended credit freely, built their own sloops and ships to open trade routes with southern Europe, dealt in both crops and slaves, and offered new markets to small farmers. In the 1770s, this was modified only by the appearance of Philadelphia firms, which took over the long-distance trade. With their smaller vessels, the great families remained in control of the regional credit structure and served as mediators between Kent County's farmers and the Philadelphia merchants. In this way, Chestertown remained involved in Atlantic trade.

A grandee was the top of the colonial elite—a man who was used to being respected within his local community. Chestertown came to be dominated by its merchant-planters, who built multistoried brick houses that were furnished in luxury and surrounded them with numerous outbuildings. Their plantations now became places of leisure and retirement as well as productivity. As grandees, their degree of conspicuous consumption separated them from the rest of society, and they were rewarded by patronage positions in the colonial government.

THE FAMILIES

In the mid-seventeenth century, families of modest fortune migrated to Kent County from Virginia, England and the Western Shore. The names of the heads of these founding families are familiar: Thomas Smyth, Thomas and William Ringgold, Thomas and Joseph Hynson, Joseph Wickes, Emory Sudler. Many of their original homes were modest. Not until the eighteenth century would some of their descendants become grandees and face the conflict caused by the movement for independence.

The Ringgolds

Thomas Ringgold, Thomas Smyth, Thomas Hynson and Joseph Wickes came to southern Kent County from Kent Island in the 1650s. The Ringgold family dated to Major James Ringgold, who held Huntingfield, a grant of 1,200 acres at the mouth of the Chester River. Here he established the early county seat of New Yarmouth—named for his ancestral home—where the settlement was laid out prior to 1680. Along the Chester River and its tributaries, the Ringgolds' land became settled up to Crumpton at Collister's Ferry. In 1722, a brick house was built at Huntingfield. Thomas Ringgold IV was a leading slave dealer. He and his brother and partner, William Ringgold, gained control of Kent County's credit in the 1770s by acting as mediators between the farmers and major credit suppliers in Philadelphia.

Trumpington, built circa 1780, was the home of Thomas Smyth III. Smyth was able to hold on to Trumpington when his fortunes declined after the Revolution. *Kent County Historical Society.*

The Smyths

In the 1680s, Thomas Smyth settled on Kent Island. In 1687, he purchased Trumpington, with a Chesapeake frontage, on the Eastern Neck, the extreme end of Kent County where the Chester River joins Chesapeake Bay. When it was first surveyed in September 1658, the original grant contained four hundred acres. Smyth died in 1710 and left his property, including Trumpington, to his son, Thomas II, and daughter, Martha. Thomas II married Mary Ann Ringgold, and when Mary Ann died in childbirth, he remarried to Mary Frisby, thus tying the Smyths to two of Kent County's leading families. The early Smyths served in a number of political capacities and were members of the St. Paul's Parish vestry.

The Sudlers

A merchant, Emory Sudler came into partnership with Thomas Smyth III after marrying Smyth's half sister, Martha. In 1767, Sudler partnered with

Smyth to build and own the 160-ton *Friendship*, with a carrying capacity of over seven thousand bushels of wheat. It sailed to the Iberian Peninsula, making two voyages a year to Cádiz or Lisbon. Martha brought with her a portion of the Radcliff Cross estate, where the couple built a house about 1770. Three years later, Sudler represented Kent County in the Provincial Assembly. From 1771 to 1785, Sudler owned the Buck property at Queen and High Streets in Chestertown. Sudler's fortunes clearly depended on his relationship with the Smyth family.

The Hynsons

The Hynson family and three servants came from England and first lived on Kent Island. In 1659, Thomas Hynson was granted Hinchingham manor, a 2,200-acre estate lying along the shore of Chesapeake Bay and extending north from Swan Creek. He was thirty-nine years old at the time and so well liked by the Calverts that he had already been made high sheriff of Kent County. However, in 1660, he supported Governor Josias Fendall's effort to abolish the Upper House in favor of the Lower House of the Maryland Assembly. The Calverts put down the rebellion, and Thomas was exiled to Eastern Neck Island. With his friend Joseph Wickes, he received grants and acquired land for the entire island, a total of 3,600 acres. In 1730, Thomas Hynson Jr. built a gambrel-roof house, called Hynson's Division, on his portion of the island.

The Wickeses

From the Isle of Wight and Lower Norfolk Counties in Virginia, the Wickeses left with a group of Puritans in 1650 and settled in Kent County. In 1658, a joint grant was issued to Joseph Wickes and Thomas Hynson for eight hundred acres. This estate, named Wickcliffe, was located at the extreme end of Eastern Neck Island, its shores being washed by the Chester River. Thomas Hynson's heirs surrendered their rights to the property to Joseph in later years for a consideration. In 1656, Joseph was appointed a justice of the peace for Kent County. Twenty years later, he served with John Hynson and Cornelius Comegys on the Kent County Court. As vessels came into the Chester River, they passed close to the Wickes house, where Lambert Wickes, the future rebel naval commander, was born in 1735. In

1740, Joseph Wickes III and his wife, Mary Piner, built a modest wood-frame house for their farm at Piner's Grove, near Chestertown.

The Carvills

From Salter's Load, Norfolk, England, Thomas Carvill first settled in St. Mary's County, Maryland, and then moved to Kent County in the 1680s. In 1694, his son, John, was granted a mere twenty-six acres, called Carvill's

Carvill Hall, built circa 1695. John Carvill erected this exceptionally large brick house on Carvill's Prevention during a time when most plantations were modest frame buildings. *Kent County Historical Society.*

Prevention, on the shores of Fairlee Creek. One year later, he began to build the house that stands there today. At the time, it was a most elaborate home—a two-and-half-story brick structure in Flemish bond. The steeply pitched gable roof ends and two-foot overhang at the eaves attest to its age. Sometime in the eighteenth century, a one-and-a-half-story addition was built to serve as the kitchen.

John Carvill was prominent in Maryland politics during the last decade of the seventeenth century and the first decade of the eighteenth century. Significantly for Chestertown, in 1708, he was appointed to a commission charged with "erect[ing] a port and town…at the Chester Ferry at or near the place where the old courthouse stood." He was also a burgess to the General Assembly from St. Mary's County in 1692 and from Cecil County six years later. From 1694 to 1696 and again in 1699–1700, he was high sheriff of Cecil County, the most lucrative and powerful position in the county. Still, he refused the position in 1702. Four years later, the modern boundaries of Kent and Cecil Counties were established, making Carvill a resident of Kent County. From 1708 to 1711, he represented Kent County in the General Assembly. Locally, he was a member of St. Paul's vestry until his death in 1709.

The Comegyses

Cornelius Comegys came from Virginia to Maryland in 1663 and received his first grant of four hundred acres. As an immigrant, he petitioned the Maryland Assembly in 1671 to be made a naturalized citizen. In his petition, he states that both he and his wife, Millimety, were born in the Netherlands. Cornelius II, their eldest son, was born in Jamestown, Virginia, in 1659, while their other children—Elizabeth, William and Hannah—were born in Maryland. Several thousand acres were later acquired by Cornelius. In 1676, he was made a member of the Commissioners of Justice for Kent County. Commanding a splendid view of the upper Chester River, Presbury was built about 1710 by Alethia, daughter of the William Comegys, the second son of Cornelius. It was covered by a steeply pitched roof, and inside was considerable woodwork and great fireplaces. At the time, the property extended to the Chester River, where Collister's Ferry carried people across.

The Frisbys

James Frisby was born in England in 1651 and came to Kent County before the turn of the century. In 1704, his will provided his sons, Thomas and William, with dwelling plantations and land. Prior to 1722, William purchased a seven-hundred-acre tract of Hinchingham from the Hynsons. William, a member of the vestry of St. Paul's Parish, was a man of great prominence on the Eastern Shore. After the Puritan Uprising of 1694, the Maryland Assembly entrusted him with presenting the bishop of London and the Commissioners of Trade and Plantations a copy of the Act of Assembly, establishing the Church of England in Maryland, for their approval. In 1756, James Frisby, gentleman and son of William and Jane Frisby, purchased three hundred acres of farmland bordering the upper reaches of the west branch of Langford Bay. His first wife had been a Hynson, and his wife at the time was Rebecca Ringgold, daughter of Thomas and Rebecca Wilmer Ringgold. In 1762, the couple built a two-and-a-half-story brick house with a smaller kitchen wing. The interior was elegant, as evidenced by the fully paneled living room with glazed cabinets flanking the fireplace. In the nineteenth century, the estate became known as Violet Farm. When Rebecca died, James remarried to Margaret Moore, and in 1774, the couple built Hinchingham on the Bay, another large plantation. Like their ancestors, these Frisbys were communicants of St. Paul's Church.

From 1733 to 1769, eight Frisbys are listed as county landowners. Four of them resided in manors or held land at Hinchingham, although William Frisby of Frisby's Purchase was also found in New York. In 1738, Ann Frisby held a lot in Chestertown, and in the 1760s, Peregrine Frisby held three lots in the town.

The Lloyds

The Lloyds were unquestionably Eastern Shore grandees. Edward Lloyd had settled in Virginia's Lower Norfolk County in the 1630s. He then led Puritan settlers to the Seven River on the Western Shore and arrived at the site of Wye Plantation on the Eastern Shore in the late 1650s. In 1666, Edward returned to England to become a London tobacco merchant, leaving his son, Philemon, in charge of his Eastern Shore property. In 1697, Henrietta Maria Lloyd inherited six plantations, four along the Wye River and two inland on Tuckahoe Creek. To run them, she had thirty-two slaves, two female servants, five overseers and a workforce of twenty-three male field hands.

While most of the Lloyds' property came to be in Talbot and Queen Anne's Counties, their influence was pervasive enough for a later branch of the family to develop in Kent County. Robert Lloyd was born in 1712 and established himself in the mid-1730s on Hope Plantation in Queen Anne's County. By the 1750s, he had developed five holdings—one on

The Chestertown house of Rebecca Lloyd, daughter of Edward Lloyd of Wye House in Talbot County. This highly modified structure, built around 1733, represents the presence of the Lloyds in Chestertown.

the St. Michael's River, producing tobacco, wheat and corn—and had become the largest slaveholder on the Eastern Shore. He died in 1770 and was succeeded by Edward Lloyd IV, who was born in 1744. Edward IV also became an accomplished planter, with properties in both Talbot and Kent Counties. He held two hundred slaves to produce tobacco, corn and wheat. Reputedly, his slaves sang the following song to please the pride of the Lloyds:

> *I am going away to the great house farm,*
> *O, yea! O, yea! O, yea!*
> *My old master is a good old master,*
> *O, yea! O, yea! O, yea!*

The Kent County branch of the Lloyd family was headed by Richard Lloyd and included Edward Lloyd III's daughter Rebecca Lloyd Anderson and his accomplished son Edward Lloyd IV. Sometime after 1733, Rebecca had a brick house on High Street constructed for her. Edward was a pew holder in the Chester Parish church in 1768.

Richard Lloyd was the son of Edward Lloyd II, born in 1717. Twenty-five years later, he was a justice of inspection for Kent County's warehouses. In the colonial wars, he was a colonel of the Kent County militia. In 1772, he was a pew holder in the Chester Parish church, and eight years later, he donated grain in the failed effort to pay the salary of the parish's parson. At the end of the war, Richard held land in Coventry, Hillsdown and Fairlee. By then, the estate in Richard's hands consisted of 712 acres, twenty-one slaves, seventy-two horses, 172 cattle and 166 ounces of plate.

The Bordleys

Thomas Bordley came to Kent County from England in 1649. In 1737, his ten-year-old son, John Beale Bordley, went to live with his uncle in Chestertown, where he received his early education under the direction of the Chestertown Free School teacher Charles Peale. In 1770, Bordley married Margret Chew of Pennsylvania, providing him with a plantation on the southern half of Wye Island, where he was a neighbor of the Lloyds on the Wye River. Here he introduced an English field system, which prevented depletion of the soil. Following Kent County's trend, he turned away from tobacco and was involved in the wheat trade with Spain.

Fancy Farm, built circa 1780, was erected for a tenant by leading Queen Anne's County planter John B. Bordley. His son William was a Kent County militia colonel in the Revolution. *Kent County Historical Society.*

Like the Lloyds, John Bordley's land interests carried to Kent County. By 1783, he held 1,816 acres in Kent County in farms named Fancy Farm, Grumble, Providence, Bordley's Beginning, Coventry, Hillsdown and Harris Adventure. His son John Jr. would inherit most of these farms and eventually hold at least a dozen slaves. In contrast, his other son, William, was a Kent County militia colonel who became involved in the Revolution by trying to put down the insurrection on the lower Eastern Shore. He also operated a plantation on Wye Island, doubtless in cooperation with his father. Both sons were active in the Chester Parish. They are not to be confused with Dr. William Bordley, who resided in Chestertown.

In the late seventeenth and early eighteenth centuries, before Chestertown existed, planters came from England and Virginia and were preoccupied with work, a need to succeed materially, a competitive individuality and a concern to provide adequately for each of their sons. They needed to succeed materially before they could become leisured gentlemen.

The expansion of the Atlantic market increased the profits from tobacco planting and initiated the cultivation of wheat and corn. The natural increase of the black population added to the wealth of the planters, and as this labor force grew, the value of land rose. The stability of society was based on this prosperity. As long as the economy allowed a father to establish his sons in their own homes, they remained on the Eastern Shore. With each new generation, ties of kinship and land among families multiplied. While our sampling of these families is not exhaustive, it is enough to follow them into the eighteenth century, when they became more prosperous planters. This would lead to the development of Chestertown as a port and as a center of wealth and entertainment, a fact exemplified by its extensive waterfront mansions.

Chapter 2

Planters Become Merchants in Chestertown

In the midst of Kent County's extensive agricultural development, Chestertown was an eighteenth-century commercial creation that came to be the largest community on the Eastern Shore. It was rare in that most of Britain's southern mainland colonies did not readily produce urban centers, instead remaining largely rural. This town was a result of the plantation economy, which concentrated wealth in the countryside but required a commercial outlet if it was to succeed. Chestertown's development can conveniently be divided into in four eras: 1696–1739, 1740–63, 1764–74 and 1775–83.

THE EARLY ERA, 1696–1739

In 1706, Chestertown received help from the Maryland Assembly when it was named one of Maryland's six royal ports of entry, as it was located at the navigable head of the Chester River. The assembly picked the ports, but its choices were guided by the Crown's administrators, who wanted to establish central shipping points where they could more easily control trade and levy duties. Two years later, the Maryland Assembly authorized the purchase of "fifty acres of land at Chester Ferry near the place where the old court house stood." This land was to be "laid out and divided into one hundred lots" and to be called New Town or Chester—Chestertown after 1780. The commissioners entrusted to lay out the town included John Carvill and Daniel Pearce. Housing construction began in the 1720s. The plan was finalized in 1730, with the lots covering one hundred acres. In no way do the houses built in this era resemble the mansions that would later appear in Chestertown.

The Courthouse

The Kent County Courthouse was transferred from early New Yarmouth to Chestertown in 1696, when Chestertown was not yet settled. The first court was held in a private Chestertown home. As to the extent of its authority, the Maryland Council's order of 1707 reads, "All towns, rivers, creeks and coves in Cecil, Kent and Queen Anne's Counties (except Kent Island) shall be deemed members of Chester Town in Chester River." The original courthouse did not survive, for it was destroyed by arson around 1720. Rebuilt in the following year, the new courthouse was used until the middle of the century.

The presence of a courthouse provided economic benefits for Chestertown. Maryland's courts and officials were well paid. Court staffs were often identical to that of the vestries, ensuring the rule of the gentry. When court was in session, an influx of planters, farmers and mechanics appeared, and accommodating them proved lucrative. In 1733, Joseph Nicholson bought a Chestertown lot from John Lovegrove, a shoemaker and tanner, and constructed a five-bay, gambrel-roof structure in Flemish bond brickwork with glazed headers. This structure would become the White Swan Tavern. He and his wife ran the tavern until he died.

While it did have an early courthouse, Chestertown did not have a parish church. Typically, Anglican churches were not built in a town but rather at a central rural crossroads, facilitating travel from all over the parish. It was here that the vestry of wealthy planters met, sometimes in their own vestry house. When a house of worship was finally erected in Chestertown in 1720, it was merely an Anglican chapel of ease that belonged to St. Paul's Parish church. Anglican parish churches remained based in the countryside, where the planters had their plantations and dominated the vestries.

The port did not flourish at first, despite the status of being the official port of entry for Kent, Cecil and Queen Anne's Counties. Chestertown did have modest trade with the British sugar islands in the West Indies, where it could exchange its grain and livestock. In 1730, the Maryland Assembly appointed a new commission to renew the port, which suggested the construction of warehouses. At this time, no customhouse existed.

Maryland and Kent County were not yet great consumers of English goods. In 1733, Governor Samuel Ogle explained that the inhabitants could purchase only what they could afford to buy and that "the exceeding poverty of the people in general, occasioned by the low price of tobacco, hath driven the poor families to make some few course woolens and linens, to cloth themselves, without which they must go naked." At this time, Maryland's small farmers were forced into home manufactures because they could not afford to be consumers.

The Middle Era, 1740–63

Chestertown profited during the colonial wars because the British war fleets that patrolled the Atlantic coast required provisioning. Ship captains contracted for supplies with local merchants and paid in written drafts on British agencies, which took time to be redeemed. Additionally, the presence of the Royal Navy minimized the depredations of privateers and pirates, reducing shipping risks and lightening freight charges. The colonial wars also opened up Chestertown to the possibilities of Atlantic trade.

By mid-century, Chestertown had become a flourishing port. The Atlantic route took its shipments out of Chesapeake Bay bound for the Caribbean or Southern Europe and, more rarely, the British Isles, New England or West Africa. It was this trade that focused on tobacco while a second regional route developed around the grain trade. The grain went north to Head of Elk, where it was shifted to wagons for the overland trip to Christian Bridge, Delaware. From there, it was shipped out to the Delaware River and up to Philadelphia, where it was reexported. In addition to the British factors, Philadelphia merchants appeared on Chestertown's streets and purchased town lots and nearby plantations.

In the 1730s, it is possible a customhouse existed in a small brick building on or close to the great wharf at the end of High Street. Technically, in 1742, Chestertown was a part of the Patuxent Customs District, which included Annapolis and Oxford. Ships that left Chestertown had to put in at Oxford or Annapolis to clear customs. However, that same year, Chestertown became its own customs district, with the rector of St. Paul's, Reverend James Sterling, serving as the customs agent. Sterling had influence in London,

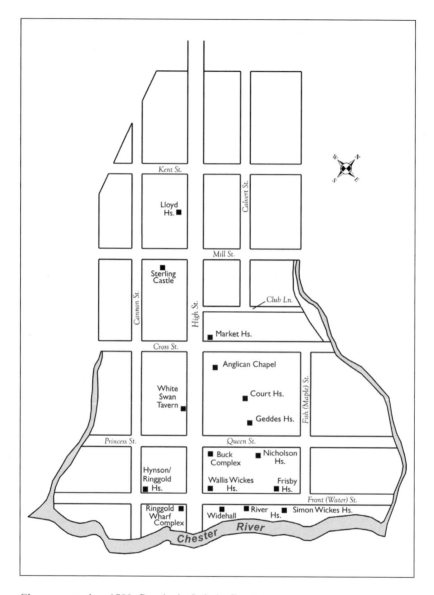

Chestertown, circa 1780. *Drawing by Catherine Escarpeta.*

and he held the lucrative position until his death in 1763. After that, two customs agents were appointed with an annual salary of 6,400 pounds of tobacco. However, problems surfaced, and the office was discontinued from 1764 to 1767. Finally, in 1767, a naval station to administer a customhouse was revived, and William Geddes was named the customs agent. The extent of the Chestertown Customs District continued to be a bone of contention in the 1770s because its boundaries had never been well defined.

Warehouses and counting houses were also signs of Chestertown's prosperity. Warehouses were built by Kent County planters as they moved to become merchants. A large merchant warehouse would be erected facing Front Street. The Maryland Assembly developed a policy of supporting public warehouses throughout each county so that the quality of Maryland tobacco could be inspected. These inspections helped eliminate poor quality and fraud and made Maryland tobacco more competitive in British markets.

In 1748, the Justices for the Inspection of Tobacco described the location of warehouses throughout Kent County. The centerpiece of their plan, erected on a half-acre lot near the Chester River, was the largest warehouse in Chestertown to be constructed with public funds. However, in 1760, the caretakers made a fire in the building and then left it untended while they went to breakfast—when they returned, the building was in flames. One attendant got on the roof to extinguish the fire but fell in and was burned to death. Along with the warehouse, seven thousand pounds of tobacco was destroyed. Such were the pitfalls of Chestertown's most extensive warehouse.

British Merchants and Factors

During the middle era, patterns of consumption on the Eastern Shore changed swiftly as English manufactured goods inundated the households of even rural farmers. They aggressively entered the consumer market, demanding amenities that richer neighbors now took for granted. In the 1740s, nearly half of all British exports went to Maryland and Virginia planters. By the 1760s, however, the Chesapeake share would fall to 30 percent as other colonies joined the rush to obtain British goods. Trade was handled by factors representing London and West Country merchant firms, which sought to obtain the best prices for the imported goods they sent to the colonies.

One group of North Devonshire merchants, in the relatively unknown community of Bideford, made an effort to supply Chestertown with imports. Bideford, along with nearby Barnstable and Appledore, formed a major trading center on the River Torridge estuary. While Bideford was by no means the only port of call for Maryland captains, it was one of several small ports that would trade directly with Chestertown. London was, of course, the dominant port of the colonial trade, but in the eighteenth century, the western ports of Liverpool, White Haven, Glasgow and Bideford also participated.

Until the 1690s, Bideford's pottery and woolen goods were traded from ships along the rivers in Maryland. From the waterways, ships returned to Bideford with cargos of "fresh, early tobacco, which fetched a higher price." By this direct trading, the North Devon port established its reputation as an importer of the best tobacco.

Some Bideford merchants found investment in Kent County land to be a promising venture. One such merchant was John Buck, whose family flourished in the late seventeenth and eighteenth centuries by trading textiles and pottery for tobacco and timber from the Chesapeake to coastal Maine. Buck never visited Chestertown, but his agent probably used a house that he had purchased there. Buck was not only a prominent merchant but also a member of Parliament. The owner of extensive land in the Chesapeake region, he was an avid participant in the transporting of convicts to Chestertown, purchasing the bonds of condemned criminals and shipping

The Buck Complex, Chestertown, built circa 1735. The Bucks, a Bideford merchant family, established an administrative, storage and retail complex to sell Bideford pottery and woolens in exchange for tobacco. They left Chestertown in 1771.

them across the Atlantic to work on tobacco plantations in Maryland in exchange for tobacco, timber and wheat.

To facilitate his trading, Buck invested in several Chestertown lots, on which he built a house and a storage building. His property, purchased in 1735 from a Chestertown mariner, was developed over the following years and stretched from Queen Street to the corner of High Street. The house on Queen Street was eventually advertised for sale as a possible storeroom and "compting-house." It was probably built as a residence for the family factors or trade representatives. The larger dwelling on High Street was sold in 1768 completely furnished. In between the two properties were a commodious stable with nine stalls, a yard with a good well and new pump and "other conveniency fit for a gentleman's family in private life or public business." A house of the era, it is practical rather than embellished. It is not likely that the Bucks would have needed a shop; rather, as noted, they would simply have traded from their ships.

John Buck died in 1745, but his sons, William and George, continued the business in Chestertown. The two heirs advertised the complex for sale in 1768. They may have been upset by the Stamp Act riots three years earlier, but these events had little effect on Chestertown's trade. The brothers sold their property to Emory Sudler, the brother-in-law of Thomas Smyth. The sale of the Buck complex in 1771 signified the passing of the middle era, when factors were crucial to trade with the British Isles.

Planters as Merchants

Planter families came from the countryside to Chestertown, and some built larger houses than at their plantations and farms. At first, this was a matter of making households fit for business, as planters required a building that went beyond domestic space and contained storerooms, granaries, cooperages, ropewalks, accounting rooms and shops. Inside these houses, family comfort was not a priority, as business acumen and family strategies complemented each other.

The Ringgold family began to buy real estate in Chestertown in the 1720s and 1730s. Thomas Ringgold IV made extensive investments there. Until his death in 1772, he was Chestertown's most respected attorney and merchant. He represented Kent County often in the Maryland Assembly and was in the vestry of St. Paul's Parish and, after 1766, the newly formed Chester Parish. With his brother William and son Thomas V, he formed a firm combining bookkeeping with banking and trade.

The Ringgold Complex, Chestertown, built circa 1745. Samuel Massey erected this house, which was purchased and enlarged by Thomas Ringgold IV before 1772 and used as a combined residence and business property.

In 1749, to serve as a center for his enterprises, Thomas Ringgold purchased the extensive wharf property that merchant Samuel Massey had begun to develop four years earlier. The building featured Flemish-bond brickwork with glazed headers and a basement floor that held granaries and storage areas. Sometime before 1772, Thomas constructed an addition, similar to the original structure, facing the river. The property also contained several outbuildings.

At Thomas's death in 1772, his son Thomas V gave a portion of the structure to his mother, Anna Marie Earle Ringgold, to be used as her residence and provided instructions for continuing the firm's enterprises. Spaces were to be rented on the best terms; these included a dry goods store and computing house—as well as the cellars and vaults underneath them—a cooper's shop on the two wharves and large granaries and storehouses on the wharf. The only resident, Anna Marie, was protected from the tenants by a yard around her kitchen door. Unfortunately, Thomas V died only two years after his father, so it is unclear how successful these enterprises were.

William Ringgold, the brother and partner of Thomas IV, made his home in another Ringgold house on Front Street and had a wharf behind it. A relative, Thomas Smyth III, had begun this house in the late 1750s and sold it to Peregrine Frisby in 1760. Four years later, William purchased the property from Frisby. Ringgold added on to the house on the riverside, where the cove was filled in and replaced by terraces. He was also responsible for the work on the Chestertown Chapel of Ease, completed in 1772. He rented pews in both this church and the Worton church, thus covering all of Chester Parish.

The Courthouse Expanded

The earlier courthouse had deteriorated by 1750. At the request of the justices, the General Assembly authorized fifty thousand pounds of tobacco as capital to build a new one. It would be an apsidal-ended courthouse, now set in the center of the public ground with the Anglican chapel in one corner and the churchyard covering the rest. In the late eighteenth century, a jail, about the same size as the renovated Anglican chapel, stood behind the courthouse.

The Late Era, 1763–74

Similar to Annapolis on the Western Shore, Chestertown became the center of the Eastern Shore's social world. Chestertown was noted for its culture—accounts tell of scientific lectures, bookshops and performances of Shakespeare. Chestertown was now the largest place on the Eastern Shore, with 130 houses, or about seven hundred inhabitants. It was a place of conspicuous consumption, fueled by merchant and gentlemen planters who wanted to show off their wealth. These planters were given the recognition of grandees or leaders of society.

Mania for Consumer Goods

A circa 1760 oil portrait of Lucretia Leeds, shown wearing a gown of expensive silk or satin. The use of fabric is accentuated by her free-hanging cuffs. Ruffles and lace were sewn to the bodice, while the satin bow was a popular decoration. *Kent County Historical Society.*

In 1771, William Eddis of Annapolis noted that "the quick importation of fashions from the mother country is really astonishing. I am almost inclined to believe that a new fashion is adopted earlier by the polished and affluent American than by many opulent persons in [London]." Eddis felt that all of Maryland's classes of people were willing to work diligently to obtain superior English manufactures. It was ladies from old families like Lucretia Leeds who spent the most. Lucretia was a descendant of William Leeds, who had come to Kent Island in the 1650s and in 1661 served as Kent County's representative to the Proprietary Assembly.

In the 1760s, a simple gown required extravagant amounts of imported silk or satin fabric to form voluminous free-hanging cuffs. Another example of such mania is the quilt, which by the end of the eighteenth century had moved from being rare and only for the best households to being a common feature of middle-class households. The earliest colonial quilts were not economical, practical or especially warm; rather, they were a luxury item by which an owner could claim high social status. The quilts were cut from large blocks of fabric designed for a formal effect. The bed was the focus of quilt design, with children often sleeping on quilts under their parents' bed. No odd pieces of old fabric were used here; new fabric was purchased specifically to make the quilt. You had to have manufactured fabric to make these quilts (homespun would not do). The fabric was manufactured in the British Isles and exported by English merchants, who brought it to Chestertown.

John Hewson chintz fabric. In the 1780s, chintz was available from Philadelphia merchants and popular with quilt makers. Hewson brought his skills as a fabric printer when he emigrated from England in 1774. *Author's collection.*

Women were directly involved in fashioning the fabric into a quilt—even on plantations, where they had to manage a workforce of slaves.

A Kent County survey shows that in 1710, only 10 percent of male slaveholders had quilts, denoting that only the wealthiest slaveholding households had them. This changed in the next century, for by 1820, 63 percent had them. The consumer revolution had spread from the elite planters to the middling sort, who now owned 82 percent of all quilts. Quilt frames were found only in households with slaves, indicating that quilting was still limited to slaveholding households—although this meant at least half of the households in Kent County. Overall, there were not enough quilt frames to produce all of Kent County's quilts, evidence that some must have been quilted outside the home or purchased ready-made from a shop or ship that carried English imports.

Grandees Build Mansions

In a sense, a gentleman could be a grandee only if he had a house in Chestertown. The two grandee families that dominated Chestertown's waterfront real estate were the Ringgolds and the Smyths. They did receive minor support in filling in the lots from relatives like the Frisbys, Samuel Wallis and, very late in 1780, the Wickes.

The aforementioned Ringgolds were still in the thick of trade in the early 1770s. Thomas Ringgold IV ordered and received British goods from an Annapolis merchant who resided in London. In Chestertown in 1767, Ringgold had acquired the house that Dr. William Murray had built in 1743, on property purchased from planter Nathanial Hynson, and it became known as the Hynson-Ringgold House. Ringgold, who had admired the house from his wharf home, remodeled and extended the main block, installing a paneled north parlor in the front section around 1771. Two years later, George Washington visited the Chestertown waterfront and "dined on

The Hynson-Ringgold House, Chestertown, built circa 1743. The front section was built by Dr. William Murray and purchased by Thomas Ringgold IV in 1767. The purchase allowed the Ringgolds to control much of Chestertown's waterfront.

board the Annapolis at Chester Town & supped & lodged at Mr. Ringgolds."
His hosts were Thomas V and Mary Galloway Ringgold. When completed,
the Ringgold estate covered much of the riverfront block of Front Street,
from his wharf property to the Hynson-Ringgold House, and included
outbuildings such as stables, smokehouses and counting houses.

Thomas Smyth III

In the 1760s, Thomas Smyth was already a wealthy merchant, shipbuilder
and legal expert who resided on the family estate at Trumpington. He had
been born in 1730 at one of his father's plantations. When his father died
in 1741, it was stipulated that Thomas should study law with lawyer James
Calder. Thomas was married at St. Paul's in 1752, and Thomas Jr. was born

Widehall, Chestertown, built 1769. Erected by merchant Thomas Smyth III, this structure
was named for its expansive second floor. During the Revolution, it was a center of Smyth's
activities in support of independence, but he lost the house after the war.

a year later. In 1764, he was a sheriff of Kent County and judge of the county court. He was in business with Emory Sudler, his brother-in-law, who shared with him the common problem of runaway servants.

Having petitioned the assembly because of a lost deed, Smyth was granted a lot on Front Street. Purchasing the lot in 1769, he began construction of Widehall a year later. He built from the ground up using architect Howard Sill and Philadelphia artisans. The commodious and formal house was a result of conspicuous consumption.

About the same time, in 1766, James Frisby Sr. had a house built on Front Street among his relatives' houses. Uniquely, the Frisby house was modest compared to the others on Front Street. It had a simple three-part brick

Frisby House, Chestertown, built 1766. This modest brick house does not reflect the fact that the Frisbys were wealthy grandees.

façade and was the only dwelling on the town side of Front Street, the area usually reserved for the gardens and outbuildings of the waterfront houses. After all, the Frisbys did not become merchants and had no direct need for a wharf; they seemed to have wanted only to be near their relatives.

Even with the development of the waterfront real estate, not all was perfect in Chestertown. Its port faced difficulties. A report filed by an inspector general in 1770 noted that Chestertown had been steadily declining in the number of ships that passed through its customs so that the annual number was only twenty. Its consumer base was limited to the northern Eastern Shore, certainly smaller than that of a port like Annapolis or Philadelphia. The Chester River had an average depth of only sixteen feet, too shallow for fully laden ships. Its shipbuilding industry was thus limited to sloops with a small cargo space.

Chestertown now had competition within Kent County. With sixty houses and a considerable German population, Georgetown, on the Sassafras River, was the second-largest community in the county. It was also home to a ferry that crossed the Sassafras River, facilitating north–south travel. Georgetown was located along the route for wheat that was sent to the Philadelphia market by way of Delaware's Appoquinimink and Duck Creeks into the Delaware River.

THE WAR, 1775–83

When the war came, the age of conspicuous consumption almost disappeared as the vital trade of Chestertown's waterfront was disrupted throughout the conflict. Chesapeake Bay was closed to shipping, unless a captain had the nerve to run against the British gauntlet. If confronted, the contest was uneven, and the enemy usually won. However, it was not just the ships of the Royal Navy that prevented Chesapeake trade but also a host of Loyalist privateers and armed barges. Still, trade did not die during the war for two reasons: the Philadelphia connection remained viable and modest profits could be made by supplying the military efforts of Congress and Maryland. With existing connections to Philadelphia merchants and the Continental military depot at Head of Elk, Kent County's planters and millers survived. Many who served as militia officers found that they were not successful in commanding men in the field but instead excelled in gathering supplies and offering contracts for the produce of Kent County plantations and farms. By the middle of the war, the Maryland legislature had placed embargoes on Kent County's wheat and foodstuffs to make certain it went to the military, although tobacco production was revived because it could be sent to foreign markets to earn exchange.

Despite Chestertown's productive hinterland, other places had more advantages in the race for military contracts. Annapolis did not have such a hinterland, but as the seat of the Maryland government, it became a military depot to rival Head of Elk, and its merchants obtained the lion's share of lucrative state contracts. At times, Chestertown and Annapolis were in the same boat. At the beginning of the war, a statewide survey showing the locations of crucial blacksmiths revealed that neither place had one. In Chestertown's case, however, Kent County's Georgetown had one, probably because it offered better access to firewood needed for charcoal in the smithy. Regardless of such competition, it is evident that some of Kent County's merchants profited from the demands of the military.

Simon Wickes's house, built circa 1780. Built during the war on Chestertown's waterfront, this house joined those of the Ringgolds, Smyths and Frisbys in homes at the port.

Surprisingly, substantial houses were still being built in Chestertown. As mentioned, the Wickeses were late in leaving their estates to arrive on the waterfront. In 1772, Simon Wickes was a pew holder in Chestertown's renovated chapel. Six years later, he was captain of a company of Kent County militia. While war continued in 1780, Simon purchased a lot on the riverbank and half a lot opposite for "222 bushels of good merchantable wheat." Suitable to the location, the house was one story higher on the waterfront than on the street and had a wharf.

Thus, Chestertown passed through four eras of development. At the head of navigation for the Chester River, it was designated by the Maryland Assembly as a port and then the seat of a courthouse. Little happened, however, until the 1720s, when the first houses appeared. After this, brick structures were built by planters with interiors and yards devoted to family businesses that revolved around warehouses and granaries. Only after mid-century did the gentry become grandees, erecting vast and embellished houses to conspicuously show off their wealth. This was the golden age of trade, when the ships that cleared Chestertown's customhouse went to ports throughout the Atlantic. The arrival of the Revolutionary War destroyed this age of affluence.

Chapter 3

Vestry Rule Sustains the Established Church

When people decided political, social and economic issues, religion was an important motivator. It was not so much a matter of theology as the long-term institutional development of the Eastern Shore's churches.

The Anglican Church in Maryland came with the first English settlements on Chesapeake Bay in the 1630s. It remained dominant throughout the next 150 years due to support from Maryland's Provincial Assembly, guidance from its local vestries and the failure of rival dissenting, evangelical and Catholic churches. Even for the South, the Eastern Shore had a remarkably homogeneous religious environment. When the Revolution came, both rebels and Loyalists would be part of the Anglican consensus. The exception to this was the rise of the Methodist movement during the Revolution.

ANTI-CATHOLICISM SPURS THE ESTABLISHMENT OF THE ANGLICAN CHURCH

Britain's "Bloodless Revolution" of 1688 forced King James II to flee to the Continent after his failed attempt to turn England back to Roman Catholicism and led to the placement on the throne of Calvinist William III and his consort, Mary II. In 1689, Maryland Puritans, by now a substantial majority in the colony, revolted against the Calverts' proprietary government, supposedly because of its preference for Catholics in official positions of power. In July, led by Colonel John Coode, a force of seven hundred Puritans defeated the Calverts' proprietarily army. The victorious Coode and his Puritans set up a new government that outlawed Catholicism and deprived Catholics of offices. In July, a Protestant Association was formed, led by Coode. He gathered a sizeable army that marched on the capital, St. Mary's City, and his Protestant associators secured the surrender of the smaller body of the Calverts' supporters without bloodshed. The associators pledged their allegiance to William and Mary and asked that Maryland be designated a royal colony rather than a proprietary one. William obliged them, establishing a royal government dominated by Protestants.

CONTINUED REVOLUTION TO ESTABLISH THE ANGLICAN CHURCH

The Maryland Assembly continued the Puritan Revolution in 1692 by establishing the Anglican Church. The assembly passed the "Act for the Service of Almighty God and the Establishment of the Protestant Religion," which established the Anglican Church and required all households to pay an annual tax for the support of church buildings and the clergy. Each of the colony's thirty parishes had a vestry sworn to enforce laws against "treason, blasphemy, and forms of immorality like drunkenness, Sabbath-breaking, dueling and unlawful cohabitation." In exchange for this duty, each parish received a tithe of forty pounds of tobacco (or its equivalent) from each free adult male and for all slaves. The tax revenue was used solely by the Anglican Church vestries and their clergy. In 1704, an act was passed "to prevent the growth of Popery in this Province" by prohibiting Catholics from holding political office. These acts put an end to the vision of religious freedom for Catholics, Quakers and Presbyterians that the Calverts had established as proprietors. However, most other denominations could worship in public, but they did not receive tithe support. In 1715, Maryland would revert back to the Calvert family as proprietors and cease to be a royal province. But this made little difference, as the Anglican Church remained firmly entrenched as the established church.

With the backing of their vestries and the assembly, Anglican churches effectively spread the gospel. By 1776, the thirty parishes established in 1692 had risen to forty-four and the clergy from eight to fifty-three. While in Maryland's early years the Calverts had controlled the selection of clergy, they now were hired by and their livings dependent on the local vestries, made up of planters. This system made Maryland's parsons the best paid in the colonies, although some felt that it also made them more inclined to immoral behavior.

In fact, membership in the vestry of the Anglican Church was the most important source of the plantation gentry's local power, ensuring that their status would not be challenged within the community. The vestry shared many of the same personnel with the county court and functioned like a parish gentlemen's club. The gentry's control in the vestry could be overruled only by the Maryland legislature.

Sundays at Anglican churches were social meetings for the planters in which business would be transacted and their power shown by marching conspicuously into the church, often after the service had begun, and sitting in the front or in their own assigned pews. They handled church construction, taxation in support of the church, ministerial hiring, maintenance of the glebe farm and the prerogatives of running the church. They tried to get along with their parsons but were easily offended and disposed to sulking or, if they had influence with the governor, having a parson removed. They tended to be traditional on theological matters and would not tolerate the evangelical spirit found among Methodists. The vestry also oversaw relief to the poor.

St. Paul's

In Kent County, the first Anglican church was St. Peter's in New Yarmouth, the early settlement at the mouth of the Chester River that had disappeared by the end of the seventeenth century. St. Peter's was replaced by St. Paul's in Kent Parish. It was one of the first parishes established by the Maryland Assembly in 1692 for the spread of the Anglican Church throughout Maryland. Near the village of Fairlee, a church was erected as early as 1694, and while a second church may have replaced this one, it was so poorly constructed that in 1707, the vestry sued the contractor for expenses. Still existing is a brick structure, dating about 1711–12 and measuring thirty feet by forty feet with a semicircular apse on the east gable. It is the earliest continually existing Anglican Church building on the Eastern Shore. St. Paul's was a typical crossroads church, wherein the vestry dominated weekly Sunday festivities.

St. Paul's Church, built in 1711, is the oldest surviving religious structure in Kent County and the Eastern Shore. *Kent County Historical Society.*

In 1692, Kent Parish's principal freeholders and leading planters elected to the vestry for life were Thomas Smyth of Trumpington, William Frisby of Hinchingham, Charles Tilden of Great Oak Manor, Michael Miller of Arcadia, Hans Hanson of Kimbolden and Simon Wilmer of Stepney. They lived many miles from St. Paul's, as all sections of the parish had to be represented in the selection of the vestrymen. In 1720, the pew holders included Colonel Nathaniel Hynson, Colonel Thomas Smyth, James Smyth, Rebecca Wilmer, Thomas Hyson, Charles Hyson, William Frisby, James Frisby, Ann Frisby, John Hynson, William Ringgold and Charles Ringgold. In 1706, Thomas Smyth gave the parish a silver chalice and paten engraved with the initials "T.S." These leaders were clearly representatives of the best planter families.

West of St. Paul's, a separate vestry house still stands. The land was bought from Thomas Ringgold, the deed stating, "This five acres of land is bought for the benefit of air and shade to the parishioners and their horses round the church in attendance on divine service and for the building of a vestry house thereon and any other parish use whatever." The one-story brick building

St. Paul's Vestry House, built 1766. The seat of the vestry was as large as a middling brick house, evidence of the vestry's power as a religious-political organization. *Kent County Historical Society.*

was constructed in 1766 at the substantial cost of twenty thousand pounds of tobacco. Both façades are laid in Flemish bond with glazed headers, and two interior fireplaces are present. It was large enough to later be used as a courthouse, a schoolhouse and a barracks for British troops during the War of 1812.

A year after the vestry house was built, Robert Read was chosen by the vestry as rector of St. Paul's, probably on the basis of his superior education. In 1774, however, Read advertised that he could not live on his tobacco stipend, although it had been considered a high salary. He protested, "His salary being lessened in value one half by the [assembly's] Act for Support of the Clergy…he finds it necessary for support of his family to join his ministerial office to some business." This act affected all of Maryland's parsons, who sought to raise the amount of tobacco provided as salaries because the market value of tobacco had fallen so low. Read's business was a grammar school, run from his house, where he offered lessons in Latin, Greek and literature at a modest annual fee. He clearly was trying to remain in Kent County and solve his financial problems. However, after only a year, as a Loyalist, he would be forced to move to Virginia.

SHREWSBURY

Kent County's second parish was created in 1698 by an act of the Maryland Assembly that established St. Paul's and Shrewsbury (South Sassafras) Parishes for Kent County. Shrewsbury existed in 1675 in Cecil County, but when the south bank of the Sassafras River was given to Kent County, a new parish was created. By 1693, the new parish had a wood-frame structure. This building was extended in 1704–05, at which time the church's fortunes began to rise, as there was a gradual increase in the population of northeast Kent County. By 1729, the original church was replaced by a brick structure,

An artist's conception of first Shrewsbury Church, built in the early 1700s. The church served Kent County's growing northwestern section adjacent to and on the Sassafras River. *Kent County Historical Society.*

and seventeen years later, a separate vestry house was built. The church was again expanded after another decade.

Starting in the late 1750s, one of the solutions the Shrewsbury vestry used to raise income was to enact an additional tax on the parish's bachelors over twenty-five years old. Whether it encouraged them to marry is unknown. The church continued to grow, and in 1767, a new gallery was added to the building. A year later, the parishioners raised funds for and presented a neat velvet cushion and cloth for the pulpit and desk in honor of their parson, George William Forester, who had served the parish for over thirty years.

In January 1775, the vestry named Reverend John Montgomery as rector. However, Montgomery refused to take the position and soon sailed to London, an obvious confession of his Loyalism. He was replaced by Thomas Hopkins in 1779. He resigned after just two years, and the vestry was glad to see him go because he was accused of drunkenness. While the church had difficulty with its parsons, the vestry appointed a sextant, cleaning lady and clerk so that the church remained open. The vestry took over management of the glebe and ran lotteries so that the financial security of the church was better than any parish in Kent County. By the end of the war, in 1781, Reverend James J. Wilmer was the parson, and leading planter John Cadwalader subscribed to his salary.

Chester Parish

A third church that has been mentioned, Chestertown's 1720 chapel, was a mere chapel of ease for St. Paul's. In 1765, the Maryland Council passed an act creating Chester Parish out of St. Paul's and Shrewsbury. But the new parish church was not to be in Chestertown. The council authorized the purchase of two acres of land "at or near the cross roads at the place called I.U. for a parish church. The land and church were to cost not more than 130,000 pounds of tobacco." The new parish's freeholders met near the village of Worton and elected a vestry, which made plans to build the new church there and to enlarge the Chestertown chapel. This was an ambitious undertaking for a new parish, although the Chestertown chapel had its own supporters who wanted a new building.

The parish vestrymen of February 16, 1766, were Aaron Alford, Macall Medford, Joseph Rasin, Thomas Perkins, St. Leger Everett and William Ringgold. Pew holder William Ringgold was certainly the most prominent of them. As to the others, Macall Medford was a pew holder, Joseph Rasin was Kent County justice of the peace, Thomas Perkins was of the famous family of millers and Everett was a landowner. The vestry must have felt that the rural site was more accessible to numerous rural parishioners and that it allowed the opportunity to raise tithable funds among the planters. They contracted for the church at Worton, and apparently it was begun, although in 1767, the vestry accused the contractor of not building the structure's frame according to their agreement, and the structure remained unfinished.

Meanwhile, the vestry also had to renovate the old chapel in Chestertown, and the citizens of the town offered to raise their own funds so that an entirely new chapel would be constructed. In 1768, the assembly matched a £500 subscription by the citizens of Charlestown to erect a new chapel on the town's public square. However, the financial effort fell short, and by 1770, 360 pounds of tobacco was assessed to the parish to finish the chapel and enclose the burial yard. Finally, in 1772, the project was completed, but it is unclear as to whether it was a new church or merely a renovation.

In the 1770s, while in the midst of the War for Independence, the I.U. Church near Worton was also completed. The cost of the two buildings weakened the parish finances and sapped the strength of the church. The war years were not fortuitous. Between 1766 and 1775, three rectors had served both parish churches, supported by a tithe of five pounds of tobacco levied on each inhabitant and collected by the sheriff. However, after 1774, as a result of the Maryland Assembly's Vestry Act, financial support was lost, and the vestry failed to meet again until 1779. With their parson gone, it is possible the churches were closed during these years.

One of the few remaining Anglican parsons in Maryland was Reverend Samuel Keene of Queen Anne's County, who, in 1779, was invited by a renewed vestry to assume duties as rector of Chester Parish. He served only a year, leaving when the parishioners failed to pay his annual salary of eight hundred bushels of wheat. This was despite the fact that merchantable grain was collected to cover the salary and church repairs. Those who donated included Thomas Smyth Jr.; Anna, Josiah and William Ringgold; Ann, Richard and John Frisby; Simon Wickes; James Tilghman; and Benjamin Chambers. Even with their leadership, however, it is evident that Chester Parish did not yet have the economic viability of St. Paul's or Shrewsbury. Not until 1809, when the I.U. Church was derelict, did the Chestertown chapel gain priority as the Chester Parish church.

Anglican Parsons in the Revolution

During the war, Anglican clergy had to swear an oath of allegiance to the king and say prayers for him during the service. As the Annapolis Assembly became more rebellious, it required clergy to take an oath of loyalty to the cause of independence. Many Anglican parsons refused, owing to their oath of loyalty to the king taken at the time of their ordination. The oaths created a crisis of conscience for the parsons, so much so that of the fifty-three parsons in Maryland in 1776, only six remained in 1780. Those who left included Chester Parish's John Patterson and St. Paul's Parish's Robert Read—and would have included Shrewsbury Parish's John Montgomery had he come. It became impossible to consistently keep the doors of Kent County's parish churches open.

Moreover, in October 1776, the constitution of the newly established State of Maryland deprived Anglican churches of their tithable support, established by the legislature in 1692. Some suggested a compromise in which tax support for any denomination would be available. And since the Anglican Church was by far the largest, it would still get the lion's share of this revenue.

In 1779, the Maryland Assembly passed the Vestry Act, meant to enhance the vestries so that churches without Anglican parsons could be reopened and religion could flourish anew. The act transferred the ownership of the individual parish from the Anglican Church to the parishioners, meaning, of course, the vestry. Previous to this, while the vestry selected new parsons, it needed the consent of the governor to install them. Now the vestry was given complete authority over the selection. The act allowed the Anglican parishes to retain titles to lands and buildings instead of having them forfeited to the state. Thus, the Anglican Church remained favored through the Revolutionary assembly's support of the vestries.

Evangelists in Revolutionary Maryland

During the Revolution, the neighboring Virginia grandees, who had long viewed themselves as models of English gentlemen, found themselves impelled not only to defy British authority over taxes but also to oppose the threat of evangelism to their vestries. Thus, in Virginia, "evangelism began as a rejection and inversion of customary practices," while the independence movement "initially tended toward a revitalization of ancient forms of community." In the Maryland vestries, the grandees and gentry sought to stem the tide of evangelism.

KENT CIRCUIT

Methodist itinerant preachers appeared on the Eastern Shore in the 1770s, bringing evangelism to the region. This upset the vestries and Anglican clergy, as the freewheeling practices of these preachers emphasized on-the-spot conversion without tax or traditional theological obligations. The scorn of Methodist preachers for vanity made them natural opponents of the planters. Still, in 1773, two Methodist societies existed in Kent County, one at John Randle's house near Worton and the other at Charles Carvill Hynson's near Rock Hall, which had a nearby Methodist meetinghouse called Hynson's Chapel. The Hynsons, of course, were an old Kent County family, and Charles's home was Bungay Hill. Late that year, itinerant William Walters was preaching in Kent, Cecil and Queen Anne's Counties. A year later, a separate Kent Circuit was formed for the three counties, serving 253 Methodists. By 1775, from Queen Anne's County, circuit itinerants made their way into Caroline County at Greensboro and, two years later, into Talbot County. Overall, the Kent Circuit now extended from the Elk River in Cecil County to the headwaters of the Nanticoke River in Sussex County, Delaware.

In addition to their evangelism, Methodist itinerants welcomed both blacks and whites to their preaching. In 1784, Methodists joined the Quakers in supporting the abolition of slavery. Some historians have considered Methodist support of abolition as contributing to the Revolutionary cause, but it was regarded as an abomination by the planter class. Rebel leadership in vestries linked Methodism to the type of foolhardy emancipation that Lord Dunmore conducted early in the war. The Methodist reforms attracted the poorer elements of society, whom the vestries felt could be easily persuaded to support the cause of the king. Figures for membership in the Eastern Shore's Methodist congregations in the 1770s and 1780s show that almost one out of every three Methodists was black. In Cecil County, the Methodist membership was almost evenly split between whites and blacks. Even more striking was the recognition that the few Methodist planters who taught their slaves the Bible had nothing to fear from them—that, in the words of Phoebe,

Bungay Hill, built in 1757, was home to Charles and Phoebe Hynson, who welcomed Methodist itinerants and felt that Methodism helped them manage their slaves. *Kent County Historical Society.*

Charles Hynson's wife, Methodist slaveholders "could leave every kind of food exposed and none [was] taken by" the previously thieving slaves.

Among the Methodist preachers, pacifism and refusal to take oaths led to persecution. From the rebel standpoint, anyone who refused to swear an oath to Congress was automatically considered an enemy, as no idea of a loyal opposition existed. The Maryland government's loyalty oath was different from other states because it required not only allegiance but also that one swear to bear arms. In 1776, at a gathering in Hynson's house near Rock Hall, itinerant preacher Thomas Rankin explained that Methodists did not take up arms and that "if we are called to suffer on this account, we will suffer for conscience sake." Four years later, Samuel Porter, commander of the militia in Caroline County, reported to the Maryland Council that when prospects "embrace the Methodist faith, [the people] change their attitude toward war" and oppose it.

Many itinerants were cast as Loyalists even though they tried to maintain a more neutral position. Methodism was a reform within the Anglican Church, and it retained its ties with that church during the war. After hesitation, John Wesley, the English founder of Methodism, had decided to support the Crown and the English Constitution, decrying independence. Most of the preachers, like Francis Asbury, Wesley's handpicked envoy to the colonies, retained their British citizenship and tried to avoid the independence movement, accepting

Freeborn Garrettson, an itinerant Methodist preacher who was accosted by a mob on his way to Chestertown in 1778. The confrontation nearly cost him his life. *General Commission on Archives and History, United Methodist Church.*

shelter from Loyalist and rebel alike. Rebels never accepted a neutral position and quickly classified Methodists as Loyalists in disguise.

The Methodist outdoor spiritual meetings were said to be contrary to the best interests of the rebel cause and some of the sermons supposedly seditious. Methodists retorted that they had been forced to make use of churchyards because the vestries of Anglican churches had shut them out, even though they scrupulously avoided preaching when Anglican services were scheduled. In 1777, grandee William Paca claimed that on the borders of Queen Anne's and Caroline Counties, "scoundrel Methodist preachers" had led an insurrection. What Paca was really complaining about was the successful development of the Kent Circuit and the spread of its message.

On the Eastern Shore, the most renowned of the Methodist itinerants was Freeborn Garrettson. Born in 1752 into a slaveholding family in western Maryland, Garrettson manumitted his slaves when he converted to Methodism. This act may have been despised by the gentry, but Garrettson said that his heart bled "for slave-holders, especially those who make a profession of religion." From 1775, he traveled throughout the Eastern Shore, spreading Wesley's message to all levels of society and putting his own life at risk. He was arrested in several places but undauntedly traveled from one hot spot to another, preaching the Methodist gospel.

EVANGELISM AMBUSHED

On June 24, 1778, while on his way to Chestertown in northern Queen Anne's County, Garrettson's religious beliefs nearly cost him his life when he was accosted by a band of opponents led by former judge John Brown. Brown tried to arrest Garrettson, seized his bridle and began striking him on the head and shoulders with a stick. Brown was aided by his servants and militiamen, who carried a rope to hang Garrettson. The judge and his followers pursued Garretson, who was ultimately thrown from his horse and knocked unconscious. An elderly lady interceded on Garrettson's behalf and brought him to a nearby house, where he recovered.

When Brown again tried to arrest the revived Garrettson, the preacher lectured him on his imminent damnation and persuaded Brown to read the scriptures. Brown was soon convinced that Garrettson was a man of God and subsequently freed him. This singular act of violence near Chestertown was stimulated by religion, not politics. The heated crowd may have been approved by some Anglican vestry members who saw evangelism as an anarchist undermining of their authority.

A double standard existed when rebel committees tried suspected Loyalists. Methodists and Quakers often received heavier fines than did other supposed Loyalists. Isaac Atkinson, an avowed Loyalist, was jailed fewer times than Freeborn Garrettson. The Methodist preacher's speaking out against slavery was regarded as more dangerous than overt Loyalism. Mixing with blacks and pacifism were seen as being more perilous to the social order than simply supporting the king.

Overall, an Anglican consensus among the three parishes that covered the county existed until the Revolution. Religious uniformity was joined to ethnic homogeneity. And while prayers for the king were required as part of the liturgy, this Anglican Church was not an import from England but a creation of the Maryland legislature, where no concept of separation of church and state existed. Beginning in the 1690s, the legislature provided Anglicans with revenue from the heads of all parish households and put vestries of laymen in charge of their operations. The vestries collected the revenue from the tithable, built and maintained the church properties, hired the parsons and cared for the poor. The planters built vestry houses separate from the sanctuary to serve as the clubhouse of an illustrious group. When the vestry attended church, they entered just before the service began, meandering toward their rented pews after having conducted business and social pleasantries in the churchyard. Clearly, the vestries were bastions of the Kent County gentry.

When the Revolution came, cracks began to appear in this seemingly tranquil façade of Maryland's Anglican Church. The educated parsons, hired by the vestry, were respected for their leaning, but not when their views clashed with the worldly ethos of vestry. When the parsons made a point of saying prayers for the king and actively supporting Loyalism, they lost the respect of their vestry and left during the Revolution. Still, the seventeenth-century parish system of vestries would endure the Revolutionary War and would even be protected by Maryland's government.

Middling and lower members of Anglican churches were tired of the vestry's aristocratic antics and were less than enthusiastic about the government's mandatory tithes eating into their pocketbooks. They were not about to overthrow the vestries' control, but they did seek to reform it. And it was here that the influence of Methodism emerged as a threat to the power of the vestries. To the gentry who sat in the vestry, Methodists were Loyalists because they were evangelistic, would not bear arms, encouraged blacks to join them and ultimately called for the abolition of slavery. It was Methodists, not Quakers or Presbyterians, who would challenge the Anglican consensus.

Chapter 4

Middling and Lower Orders

Eighteenth-century society was ranked into upper, middling and lesser sorts. The orders represented the economic, religious, political and social convictions that determined how society functioned. In Kent County, the orders were not very fluid, and opportunities to rise were few; in other words, you remained in the status into which you were born. It also meant that the safety valve to prevent unrest was to leave the Eastern Shore for greener pastures.

This lack of social mobility was due to the fact that immigration had declined at the end of the seventeenth century. While immigrants still came, they also readily left because of the lack of opportunities. In 1697, before the establishment of Chestertown, Governor Francis Nicholson wrote that the reason the inhabitants were leaving Maryland was due to the "encouragement which they receive from New Jersey, the Carolinas, and Pennsylvania. There, handicraft tradesmen have encouragement where they endeavor to set up woolen manufactures, and there is great encouragement for illegal traders and privateers, or rather pirates, which causes many men to run from the king's ships in the convoys and from merchant ships." He had accounts stating "that over one hundred seamen have left this fleet." Thus, Kent County's middling and lower orders were not increased by a flow of immigrants, and as noted, ethnic and religious homogeneity became the norm.

Still, one could enjoy his condition in the existing social structure. Modest farmers were the backbone of Kent County's economy and would go on to become Revolutionary leaders. A few became as prosperous as the gentry. At the beginning of the eighteenth century, the planters had an average workforce of seventeen slaves and annual income of well over £100 but still accounted for only 15 percent of the tobacco in market. In fact, the smaller farms of the middling sort, with only a few slaves, accounted for 22 percent and lowly servants for 44 percent of the market. Tenants accounted for an additional 10 percent. While these figures would change moderately in the eighteenth century, the fact was that the wealthy plantation gentry produced no more than a small percentage of the tobacco. They had to work with the middling farm owners to secure enough tobacco for export.

For tenants it was the longer the lease, the higher the rent. The rent was in terms of tobacco, and the best land was for the annual tobacco crop. The tenants were usually married and often had children, who could become assets after they grew up. By the mid-eighteenth century, close to half of the free adult males in Kent County were tenants. This situation developed essentially because these farmers found that they could not accumulate enough cash to purchase a freehold. Besides, landlords like the Calverts were paternalistic, and the long leases they offered were quite attractive. Still, the fact that periodic rent had to be paid reduced the amount of capital that such families could accumulate.

Gentlemen planters broke up substantial portions of their estates into medium-size farms so that middling farms were collectively the most productive sector of the farming population. The chief difference between such smaller farms and the plantations became their labor forces. Early in the century, labor in middling farms consisted of the family unit, four or five servants and perhaps two slaves. The decline in the number of servants arriving led to an expansion in the use of slave labor on the middling farms, just as it did on the plantations. Because the middling farms produced the tobacco and wheat staples, they were also tied to the outside market, which involved them not just as producers but also as consumers.

The middling farm family could buy household furnishings, repair farm buildings and purchase a little hard liquor or Madeira wine and fine linen. However, the middling family had very little capital to buy more land, add slaves or buy additional livestock. This farmer was always balancing the comfort of his family against the potential return on such investments.

The Lambs and the Perkinses

The Lambs were middling farmers; they were never confused with the great planters. Pearce Lamb came to Kent County with the first settlers. In 1683, he obtained a grant for Lamb's Range, and eleven years later, he obtained another grant, which he named Lamb's Meadows. These two tracts were in the possession of Pearce Lamb's son, Francis, when he married Rosamund Beck at St. Paul's Church in 1714—despite the fact that the Becks were Quakers. In about 1730, Francis began construction of the house, which, along with a 1753 kitchen addition, featured a gambrel roof and superior brick masonry and workmanship.

The Perkins family came later to Kent County and was also part of the prosperous middling sort. Like the Lambs, they never moved to Chestertown, although they did invest in lots that they sold to others. White Horse Farm was the home of four generations of the Perkins family, beginning with Daniel Perkins, who died in 1744. Earlier, in 1710, Perkins had acquired the milling rights at the head of Morgan Creek. Instead of hiring himself to a plantation mill, he was his own millwright and also a stonecutter. In 1721, he built a one-and-a-half-story brick house, and sometime before 1778, it was expanded, doubling the size. He may also have run a tavern on his property.

Lamb's Meadows, built circa 1730 (with an addition in 1753).

Perkins' Mills (White House Farm), built in 1721, was erected by Daniel Perkins after the establishment of the first gristmill on Morgan Creek. Daniel's sons, Isaac and Thomas, expanded the property into a milling complex. Isaac was a leading rebel in the Revolution.

When Daniel died, he could afford to bequeath the farm and mill to his son Thomas and the nearby Muddy Branch farm to his son Isaac. Thomas had four children, of which only a daughter, Mary, survived to inherit the estate in 1778. In addition to the house and mill, four frame houses, three barns, three more mills and corn, bake, milk and meat houses existed on the property. Certainly Daniel's two sons needed skill and labor to build and run this property, which was known as Perkins' Mills.

SHIP CAPTAINS AND CONSTRUCTION

Another aspect of a merchant-planter's management was that he had to hire a middling ship's captain, who often lived in Chestertown. The relationship between captains and planters made a difference in how fast a ship could be loaded and dispatched. Captains usually owned their own ships, which were products of Eastern Shore shipbuilding.

In the eighteenth century, about two-thirds of all ships built in Maryland were built on the Eastern Shore. At mid-century, Kent County ranked fourth in shipbuilding among these counties, trailing Somerset, Cecil and

Beginning in the mid-eighteenth century, Chestertown and its environs were active in shipbuilding. *Taken from Edward Hazen's* The Encyclopedia of E.A. Trades *(1837)*.

Dorchester. In the first half of the century, most ships were small, the sloop being the favorite for coastal and Caribbean traffic. By the second half of the century, the trend changed to more extensive vessels, such as schooners and snows, which were large enough for Atlantic trade. Built on speculation rather than individual request, the ships were usually sold to English merchants as much as local planters. A shipyard existed on the Chester River as early as the 1690s. Proximity to natural resources, especially lumber and wood, led most shipyards to be established outside Chestertown. However, much of the skilled labor force came from the streets of the town.

ARTISANS AND MECHANICS

While it is inspiring to think that cabinetmakers, joiners and carpenters might have come from England or neighboring colonies to embellish Chestertown, most of them, in fact, were homegrown. In 1750, twenty-three artisans owned lots in Chestertown, compared to nine doctors and lawyers and three innkeepers. Chestertown's population remained the same after the 1760s, as no great influx came to disturb the social mix. Middling farmers could afford the tools of a carpenter, joiner or cooper and needed to supplement their incomes when prices for their crops fell. Most of their tools were made in England, although they were purchased at a Chestertown store. Available were locks, H hinges, chisels, gouges, files, saws, planes and joiner's bites.

Handicrafts also appeared early, and the countryside was not as dependent on English manufactured goods as in other counties. It is possible that the development of handicrafts had little to do with Chestertown's urbanization, for most training of servants or slaves took place on plantations or farms, where weaving or pottery making needed no middleman. In the countryside, craftsmen were often also tenants and could not afford to maintain an inventory of raw materials and finished goods. Here, a lack of capital investment made it easier for boys to avoid apprenticeship and decide their own futures. Usually, however, the market still drove them to end up practicing the skills they had learned in their family. Most striking is the fact that most tradesmen who settled in Kent County also became some sort of farmer.

A small number of craftsmen brought business acumen and family strategies together, an ideal of middling families. Artisans maintained craft dynasties by apprenticing their sons and relatives so that their shops and workplaces were made of intergenerational family craftsmen. This effort, of course, kept newcomers out of the trade. The technique was especially true of trades that required start-up capital, such as millers, brewers, blacksmiths, tanners, weavers, joiners, carpenters and shipwrights. Gristmills were expensive, requiring bricklayers, blacksmiths and carpenters to build them. Shops and mills usually descended in families, and this situation was not changed by the Revolution.

Many of these craftsmen worked in Chestertown, as evidenced by the existence of a modest Pembroke table made in the 1790s by Charles Farrow, a Chestertown carpenter who signed his work, and later examples of Windsor-style chairs. On a lower level, planters required local processing by skilled craftsmen. Thus, carpenters cut timber; tanners made leather; millers ground flour, which coopers then packed into barrels or hogsheads; and shipwrights built sloops and schooners.

In Chestertown, rather modest homes existed for the middling sort. A typical structure would have two rooms with a loft, wooden floors, brick foundation piers and a brick chimney. Many also had small porches with

A circa 1800 Windsor-style chair that belonged to the Westcott family. Kent County had craftsmen capable of making such chairs. *Kent County Historical Society.*

benches astride the front entrance. One example of middling housing, dubbed "Sterling Castle" in jest because it was nothing of the sort, existed on Mill Street. This was a one-and-a-half-story wood-frame structure with two rooms, a winder staircase to the loft and an adjacent fireplace. The half-lot was sold in 1756 and the house built soon after by Robert Sterling, a lieutenant of the Forty-eighth Regiment stationed in Chestertown during the Seven Years' War. He probably could not have afforded it had he not

Sterling Castle, Chestertown, built circa 1756. A British lieutenant erected this modest house, which passed through the hands of various householders of the middling sort. The name is an exaggeration.

married Ann Scott, whose parents owed the Stephen Heath Manor. After only three years, Sterling was in debt to Bristol merchants Sedgely and Hillhouse, showing that even the middle class could live beyond its means. Richard Porter, a surgeon, then assumed the debt and received the house and its furnishings in return. Porter's wife then sold it to Emmanuel Josiah, a Philadelphia merchant, who probably used it only occasionally on visits, renting it the rest of the time. In 1771, Josiah sold the property to Ralph Storey, a Chestertown shipwright. In 1783, having left Chestertown, Storey willed the property to his son William. In capsule form, then, we see various members of the middling sort using this modest house.

THE LOWER SORT

In the 1700s, the lower sort included servants, apprentices, free blacks, slaves and even convict servants. Despite the number of indentured servants, Kent County's planters and farmers needed a still larger workforce. As we have seen, the slave trade provided white farmers with another source of labor. Enslaved blacks often performed the duty of field hands or low-skilled, dirty jobs like digging and hauling materials. They were restricted to the plantation or farm of their master and could not travel without their master's permission. More women than men labored in the master's big house. It may appear that slaves in the big house had an easier lot than those in the field. However, "fieldwork had a beginning and ending each day, but in the big house, slaves were always at the beck and call and under the watchful eye of a master."

On plantations, masters often trained male slaves in skilled trades such as carpentry, cabinetmaking, masonry and mechanics. Most of the slaves were hired out by their master, although some were permitted to earn money for themselves. Male slaves also fired the kilns used to make the bricks and then hauled bricks or gathered timber for building.

The plantation workday lasted from dawn until sunset, with the exception of Sundays, Christmas and Easter. Meals were limited to Indian corn and a bit of salt to form hominy. Child labor was common. Indentured and enslaved families frequently worked together at a subsistence level. Coupled with their grueling work schedules, few servants or slaves had adequate clothing and nutrition to help them combat disease.

Indentured servants had higher-skilled jobs, which often included making handicrafts and running a mill. Masters still worked their indentured servants intensely because owners wanted to get the most return on their money before the contracts expired. Contracted servants were voluntarily indentured, while others were convict servants. During the period of their indenture, servants were forbidden to marry, although many managed to choose mates, form unofficial marriages and have children. Childbearing, fighting or disobedience could result in a longer indenture. It is true that if punishments were too harsh or if masters did not honor the contracts, servants had the right to sue in court.

LOOKING TOWARD THE REVOLUTIONARY WAR

It cannot be emphasized enough that Maryland's grandees and leaders abhorred violence of any kind and assumed that one of the chief duties of a militia was to prevent such activities. In July 1775, the Association of the Freemen of Maryland, while supporting the creation of a rebel army, claimed to "solemnly engage in maintenance of good order and the public peace, to support the civil power in the due execution of the laws…and to defend with our utmost power all persons from every species of outrage to themselves or their property, and to prevent any punishment from being inflicted on any offenders." Anarchy, violence and class upheavals were to be avoided at all costs.

Only three major acts of violence happened in or around Kent County during the Revolution. In none of these acts were the crowds made up of runaway slaves or servants. Two of the incidents involved mobs threatening the lives of suspected Loyalists: James Chalmers was attacked in Chestertown in 1777, and as we have seen, Reverend Freeborn Garrettson was attacked near the town the following year. The third altercation took place in the countryside in 1780, when Isaac Perkins's mills were burned.

Motives are difficult to assign because few details are known about the incidents. Today, we are aware that mobs were far more organized, usually led by someone with impeccable middling credentials and traditional rather than radical in their beliefs. Usually they reacted against change, and while they threatened, they rarely harmed. The leader in the James Chalmers incident was Isaac Perkins, a middling miller who would become a leading rebel. Perkins was the captain of a Kent County militia company, and it is likely that his company made up the nucleus of the crowd. Chalmers was the local planter who wrote a treatise against independence from Britain in 1776 and who became commander of a provincial Loyalist regiment. When he retuned to Chestertown from New York early in 1777, he was attacked by Perkins's mob.

After the mob scene, Perkins spent his time harvesting and milling wheat, shipping it to Head of Elk and then having it transported to Valley Forge, avoiding the British at Philadelphia. Three years later, Perkins reported the third incident, in which his "invaluable set of mills were burned to the ground on the 27th instant at night before I reached home from Annapolis. My conjectures are that [Loyalists] in the upper part of this county [were responsible]." An active rebel, Perkins had suffered the consequences of his politics. After all, he had led the mob that attacked Chalmers. Since Perkins and Chalmers were both involved in the grain trade, it is not impossible that a personal vendetta existed between the two over flour transactions. To his credit, the respectable Perkins did rebuild his mills.

While the lion's share of the eighteenth-century written material that has survived belongs to the gentry, the middling and lower orders deserve a place in this story. Actually, modest farmers, rather than the grandees, were the backbone of Kent County's staple production. They prospered by establishing mills, granaries and handicraft production while avoiding Chestertown and the construction of great homes. Artisans in both town and the countryside maintained craft dynasties by apprenticing their sons and relatives so that their shops and workplaces were composed of intergenerational family craftsmen. Most of Kent County's craftsmen were homegrown rather than drawn from places outside the Eastern Shore.

Chapter 5

The English Constitution and *Plain Truth*

The colonies were tied to the mother country by the English Constitution, and the independence movement gradually sought to sever this relationship. The English Constitution was not a single document but rather a collection of documents and traditions that had evolved over several centuries. Its origins could be found in the distant Anglo-Saxon period, but all authorities agreed that the later Magna Carta of 1215 was one of its earlier manifestations. King John was actually forced by his nobles and clergy to sign the charter, thus limiting the power of the monarchy. A true parliament had not yet formed since simple knights and commoners were not represented in the Magna Carta. In the second half of the thirteenth century, however, Parliament began to take shape when representative commoners were invited to join the nobles and the clergy dropped out. Two houses of parliament emerged: the House of Lords and the House of Commons. The Commons claimed the crucial privilege of initiating money bills, especially taxes, and thus monarchs had to seek their consent when they were short of money. Monarchs tried to avoid calling parliaments, but in a crisis, they had to go hat in hand to the Commons because it "controlled the purse strings."

By the seventeenth century, two documents, the Petition of Right and the Bill of Rights, were added to the constitution to define the rights of Englishmen. The Petition of Right, passed by the Commons and Lords in 1628, required Charles I to desist from the illegal practices he was using to involve England in the Thirty Years' War. Charles considered the war effort to be a matter of royal prerogative, and he tried to ignore Parliament because it wanted to establish constitutional limits on his power before granting him funds. The petition, which covered several issues, prevented the monarch from taxing without the consent of Parliament, prevented prosecution of private home owners who refused to billet soldiers or sailors in their homes and reinterpreted the right of habeas corpus so that one could not be arbitrarily imprisoned. Charles tried to negotiate with Parliament over the petition but in the end grudgingly assented. The petition was thus a high moment in the growth of Parliament's power, although it claimed nothing that had not been asserted in the past and thus was thoroughly constitutional.

BILL OF RIGHTS AND THE GLORIOUS REVOLUTION

Most Whigs and British American colonials saw the Bill of Rights as the key event in the evolution of the constitution. The bill was a result of the Glorious Revolution of 1688, a relatively peaceful change in the monarchy wherein James II fled and Parliament invited William and Mary to take the throne. This gave Parliament the right to determine succession to the throne regardless of tradition and hereditary relationships. Later, the bill would inspire protesting colonists when they claimed that their rights as Englishmen had been violated. It includes familiar rights such as freedom to petition the monarch without fear of retribution, the right to bear arms for all Protestants and freedom of speech and debate within Parliament. It also declared that there would be no new taxation by royal prerogative without the consent of Parliament, no standing army in peacetime without the consent of Parliament, no Crown interference in election of members of Parliament and that the Crown could not manipulate the courts with excessive bail or "cruel and unusual" punishments.

Out of the conflict in the seventeenth century grew the idea that Britain had an ideal constitution because it balanced the three elements of government: the Crown (monarchy), the Lords (aristocracy) and the Commons (the democratic element). No one of these elements was to expand against the other, as had happened often in the seventeenth century. By the time of the Revolution, as Tom Paine noted, many felt that King George III was destroying the balance of the constitution because, through patronage, he had succeeded in providing majorities favorable to him in both the Commons and the Lords.

The only appeal beyond the constitution or Parliament was to go to the people by winning their support in an election, managing a crowd in a riot or demonstration or forming associations that would petition Parliament and the king. In fact, these activities were guaranteed by the evolving English Constitution and had been practiced in both Britain and the colonies.

During the debates over taxation of the colonies, the Commons was protective of the fact that its consent was needed for taxation. It had taken centuries to establish this constitutional right, and to subvert it was to allow the monarchy to overbalance the constitution. This is why the rebellious colonial assemblies at first tried to address the king rather than the Parliament to redress their grievances. Even after the confrontation at Lexington and Concord, many colonial protesters felt that the English Constitution, with all its flaws, was still the best form of government. Only in 1776, after reading Tom Paine, was the monarch seen as the enemy of the rights they sought.

LETTERS FROM A PENNSYLVANIA FARMER

Appreciation for the English Constitution and its traditions was alive and well in the 1760s when the colonists protested the Stamp Act and Townshend Duties on paper, glass, paint and, most famously, tea. It was against this background that John Dickinson of Pennsylvania and Delaware—a Quaker, attorney and gentleman farmer—wrote twelve letters in 1767. The letters were an immediate sensation in the press on both sides of the Atlantic, selling more pamphlets than any publication before. They were published in the popular *Maryland Gazette*, and they had a calming rather than Revolutionary effect among that publication's readers.

A circa 1860 engraving of John Dickinson by John Forest after Charles Wilson Peale. In the mid-1760s, Dickinson wrote *Letters from a Farmer in Pennsylvania*, which supported colonial protest against the policies of Parliament. *Library of Congress.*

Dickinson argued that while the colonies were in danger, the cause of liberty had "too much dignity to be sullied by turbulence and tumult" brought on by riots. Disrespect of the Crown and mother country would "injure the reputation of the people as to wisdom, valor, and virtue, without procuring them the least benefit." Petition by assemblies to the Parliament and Crown should be the principal means of protest. Hostile to any thought of independence or violence, Dickinson asserted that "the prosperity of these provinces is founded in their dependence on Great Britain."

Dickinson's Article 3 asserted that it was the undoubted right of Englishmen that no tax be imposed on them except with their own consent. Articles 4 and 5 concurred that the colonists could not be represented in the Commons and that the only taxes that could be levied on them would come by way of their own legislatures. He also discussed the relationship of the colonies within the British Empire, noting that it was administered "to [the colonies'] mutual advantage," not Britain's. Again, while the colonies should oppose the efforts of Parliament to levy taxes, they should point out their record of peaceful submission as a means of impressing British authorities. Empire and liberty were compatible.

Dickinson put his faith in the protest and the skill of colonial assemblies to check the power of their governors. The assemblies were to provide for defense, administer justice through courts and support civil government. On defense, he was concerned that even if funds were needed for important fortifications, the levying of such money still required an assembly's consent. Dickinson compared assemblymen to "Roman Senators" but feared that once an assembly had granted the requests of the Crown, they would fall into disuse, no longer playing an important role in the English Constitution. With all their imperfections, the assemblies were still the best hope of ensuring the liberty and happiness of their constituents.

In sum, Dickinson recognized that the abuse of the colonies by the Crown's ministers and Parliament had to be vigorously protested. Yet this was to be done prudently, within the framework of the English Constitution and the ability of the colonies to maintain a place in the British Empire. As long as Dickinson's views were held, no possibility of justifying independence existed. It was blueprint for protest against the arbitrary power of Parliament that would be in effect for almost a decade. But it would lead the colonies into civil war with the mother country, a consequence that Dickinson abhorred. By sticking to his principles, Dickinson's influence would remain important until 1774. But after that, he would have difficulty, as the majority of support came to favor independence.

COMMON SENSE

Thomas Paine was an English corset maker who had come to the colonies at the behest of Benjamin Franklin in 1774 and settled in Philadelphia. On January 10, 1776, Paine's *Common Sense* was published anonymously, signed "Written by an Englishman." His attack on the English Constitution was also an attack on Dickinson's letters. Paine argued that while the constitution had been necessary in the Middle Ages, which were "dark and slavish," by his time, it was "imperfect, subject to convulsions, and incapable of producing what it seems to promise." He referred to the divisions—king, peers and commons—honoring the last as being formed of "new republican materials...whose

A 1793 engraving of Thomas Paine by William Sharp after George Romney. While in Philadelphia in 1776, Paine wrote *Common Sense*, which refuted the English Constitution and called for independence. *Library of Congress.*

virtue depends upon the freedom of England." He charged the first two, by being hereditary and thus independent of the people, with overbalancing the third. The king was the most overbearing part of the English Constitution and "the power which people are afraid to trust and always obliged to check."

The monarchy did work through Parliament, but this was a mere subterfuge, for "the fate of [executed] Charles I hath only made kings more subtle—not more just." He attacked the monarchy's hereditary principle of succession, noting that it has produced "as many asses as lions." He also saw the colonies as an offshoot not just of Britain but of all Europe, noting the ethnic diversity in many colonies and calling them "free ports," able to trade their grain with any European state.

Paine felt that the only true fear of independence arose because no plan existed as to how it would function. He drew his ideas on a form of government not from the history of Britain but from nature, which he claimed created a constitution that was less likely to be disordered and easier to repair than the English Constitution. He felt that a government was a natural right and that it was "safer to form a constitution of our own...while we have it in our power." Otherwise, he warned that a Cromwell-like "rogue may hereby arise, who, laying hold of popular disquietudes, may collect together the desperate and the discontented, and by assuming themselves the powers of government...sweep away the liberties of the continent like a deluge." Paine proposed a new government for each colony thusly: "Let the assemblies be annual, with a president only. The representation more equal, their business totally domestic, and subject to the authority of a continental congress." It was an ideal that came too soon and would not have a measure of success until a decade later.

As for the reconciliation with the mother country urged by Dickinson, Paine felt that the time for it had passed, that one could not "give to prostitution its former innocence." For him, "freedom hath been hunted round the globe. Asia and Africa have long expelled her. Europe regards her like a stranger, and England hath given her warning to depart."

PLAIN TRUTH

A reader of Dickinson's popular letters was James Chalmers. In 1760, Chalmers, with several slaves and much wealth, came to Kent County, where he developed a wheat plantation on a seven-mile-long, well-cultivated island. His background was that of a British West Indies planter, having lived there since the age of thirteen. He must have brought with him an extensive library, a trait of the gentlemen planters in Maryland. Chalmers often visited Philadelphia, for as a planter, he was interested in the prices and market conditions for exporting grain. However, he was not part of Kent County's old family network.

Early in 1776, Chalmers traveled to Philadelphia, where both Dickinson and Paine were living. Chalmers would write a short book, *Plain Truth*, which he dedicated to Dickinson, who was now a member of Congress. Chalmers hoped that his pamphlet would encourage Dickinson to remain steadfast in his opposition of independence. Thus, *Plain Truth* is best seen as an update of Dickinson's earlier letters. Chalmers must have written his pamphlet in Philadelphia in March 1776. He also wrote letters in Philadelphia that supported his opposition against the independence movement. Congress was meeting there, and while he admitted that he did not know all the delegates, he venerated the majority of them and hoped he might sway them away from independence.

In the pages of *Plain Truth*, Chalmers proved to be as well educated and as well read as either Dickinson or Paine. His pen name, Candidus, was a tribute to Voltaire's *Candide*. While Chalmers believed in the freedom of the press, he knew that some authors used "the cadence of words and force of style" as "a total perversion of the understanding." Surprisingly, Chalmers did not write as an educated aristocrat to the planters of his class. Like Dickinson, he played to the middling sort. In a letter, he claimed that "the rich and high born are not the monopolizers of wisdom and virtue; on the contrary, these qualities are oftener to be found among the middling class…who, being less dissipated and debauched than those who are usually called their betters, apply themselves with more industry to the culture of their understandings."

Like Dickinson, Chalmers loved the English Constitution, which he felt, with all its imperfections, "approaches as near to perfection as human kind can bear." Following the "sublime" Montesquieu, he noted that the constitution was balanced between monarchy, aristocracy and democracy. Chalmers felt that when the Parliament was properly balanced, all was well. To him, the olive branch of reconciliation was an ever-present reality.

Unlike Dickinson and Paine, Chalmers was a student of the Bible. He admitted that "profane as well as sacred history informs us of ineffectuality of the best governments and wisest laws among a corrupt, degenerate people. This is the case in Great Britain at this day." Still, Chalmers stood up for monarchy as appearing in the Bible and by pointing to the dangers of republics. From his reading of the Bible, he concluded that "monarchy (especially a limited one such as that of England) is not inconsistent with Holy Scriptures…but that it is pleasing to the almighty, if agreeable to the people, as any other form of government." Republics always have "two parties, which divide the whole body of the people, and an eternal warfare subsists between them for power." In English history, Cromwell's Commonwealth, "after the death of the tyrant Charles…did not produce liberty—it presently ended in arbitrary power." As with Paine, Chalmers felt that republics were subject to the dangers of a dictator.

In March 1776, Chalmers wrote a letter to the people of Pennsylvania using the pen name Cato, a Roman senator much admired by the Founding Fathers. He argued that when attempts to levy taxes first surfaced in the 1760s, no legislator talked of independence; therefore, why rush into it now?

An idealized caricature of Oliver Cromwell published in 1658. Cromwell was a great captain, and thus you can see his enemies squashed at his feet. However, Dickinson, Paine and Chalmers warned that military heroes in government could become dictators like Cromwell. *Author's collection.*

The "respectable" Congress had a record of avoiding the independence issue. Chalmers sighted numerous instances of this, especially its declaration for a fast on June 12, 1775, in which they "humbly beseeched" their "rightful sovereign" to "redress" their many grievances, restore invaded rights and "reconcile with the parent state on terms constitutional and honorable to both." He noted that Maryland and even Massachusetts had expressed similar sentiments and that he could not identify any members of Congress who favored independence.

Combing through current events, Chalmers observed that neither the rebel army before Boston nor the defeated one before Quebec had "displayed...few marks of Spartan or Roman enthusiasm." He noted that it was only New England, not the middle or southern colonies, which wanted war. He questioned whether the rest of the colonies would follow New England's independence effort.

Chalmers played to the anti-Catholicism of many Founding Fathers, who were looking for European support. The "honorable" Congress would find embracing the support of France and Spain dangerous, for they were the colonies' proven enemies. He wrote, "Would you not dread their junction with Canadians and [Indians], and with the numerous Roman Catholics dispersed throughout the colonies?" He pleaded, "We remember with unsigned gratitude the many benefits derived through our connections with Britain...[and] we shudder against arming with such ardor, against the parent state rather than against France; by whom our rights, civil as well as religious, certainly were more imminently endangered."

Instead, Chalmers felt Congress should look to its friends in England. If independence was completed, it would pull the floor out from under the opposition to the ministry in England, especially leaders like Isaac Barre and Edmund Burke. He asserted, "The fabricators of independency have too much influence to be entrusted in [the task of forming a government]. This reason alone, were sufficient at present, to deter us from altering the [English] Constitution."

As to Chalmers's own Eastern Shore, he predicted that if war came, many coastal colonies would be left indefensible: "Our most fertile provinces, filled with unnumbered domestic enemies, slaves, intersected by navigable rivers, everywhere accessible to the fleets and armies of Britain, can make no defense." He concluded that those who wish true liberty should "submit by advantageous reconciliation to the authority of Great Britain" and that "independence and slavery are synonymous terms."

The greatest value of *Plain Truth* was not as a counterblast to Paine's exaggerated claims but as a description of how someone could praise Congress's efforts and yet feel that independence went too far. When independence came only three months after Chalmers expressed these sentiments, it must have been a shock to him. He would become a Loyalist as a result of the Declaration of Independence and use the ideas in *Plain Truth* to further the possibility of reconciliation within the English Constitution.

In 1776, the survival of the English Constitution in the colonies was a hot topic. A triangle of related political thought existed in the three political thinkers introduced here. Kent County's leaders must have found their ideas worthy as they debated the viability of independence.

Chapter 6

Promoting a New Government

U nlike New England, eastern and southern Maryland did not intensely feel the tax and trade restrictions from England that led to hostility against Parliament. The tobacco planters' market was in England, and it was their source of the coveted merchandise. No one wanted to disturb a good thing. As seen, many planters felt that the English Constitution was the best that mankind could devise. Loyalist James Chalmers claimed for the Eastern Shore: "The original colonists were principally English and Irish, [Roman Catholics] or of the English Church. [They] are…more interested and better disposed to remain British subjects than any other people of America." Apparently, no need for a new government existed. However, all was not well on the Eastern Shore.

PLANTER DEBT

The movement for independence began despite the fact that Chestertown and Kent County were at the height of their prosperity, sustaining a reputation as the wealthiest area of the Eastern Shore. However, this trade had the negative effect of causing Chestertown's gentlemen planters to be indebted to English and, later, Philadelphia merchants. The planter's way of life was based on the diversified production of wheat and tobacco for export and, in return, the import of luxuries from Europe. Still, the values of the grain or tobacco never covered the cost of these goods, and the planters found it impossible to cover their debts. In Chestertown, the Ringgold family firm had sums outstanding as high as £5,000 from over five hundred debtors who owed the family money. As a Kent County planter, James Chalmers explained, "A failure of commerce precludes the numerous tribe of planters, farmers and others from paying their debts contracted on the faith of peace and commerce. They cannot nor perhaps ought not to pay their debts. A war will ensue between the creditors and their debtors, which will eventually end in a general sponge or abolition of debts." But this was not the view of British merchants who sought payment.

Planter George Washington of Mount Vernon described the planters' indebted condition in April 1769 and suggested that a nonimportation agreement might provide relief, although he was uncertain of how it would be implemented in Virginia. He noted that it was "a truth universally acknowledged" that "the colonies are considerably indebted to Great Britain" and "that many families are reduced almost, if not quite, to penury and want from the low ebb of their fortunes, and estates daily selling for the discharge of debts." He felt that nonimportation of British goods was the answer to the debt problem, and he outlined a scheme by which he hoped "Gentlemen in their several counties would be at some pains to explain matters to the people and stimulate them to a cordial agreement to purchase none but certain enumerated articles out of any of the stores after such a period, nor import nor purchase any themselves." He admitted an opposition would form from the grandees, "who live genteelly and hospitably on clear estates" and "would not give up their expensive life-style. They would not consider the valuable object in view and the good of others, and might think it hard to be curtailed in their living and enjoyments." Thus, the grandee's conspicuous consumption was an impediment to nonimportation pressure on Britain.

MARYLAND NONIMPORTATION ASSOCIATION

These issues came together in Maryland about two months after Washington penned his letter, and an agreement was formed by Maryland merchants and politicians to boycott British imports. It has been analyzed as "a price-fixing agreement whose chief aim was to blackmail British merchants into selling wares at a reduced level." The idea resulted when Baltimore and

Annapolis merchants received a copy of the nonimportation agreement that Philadelphia merchants had adopted. The Philadelphians proposed that Maryland merchants form a similar association. However, when the association agreement was completed, it had so many exemptions on the goods to be boycotted that it was inoperable and was soon ignored. No record exists of participation by Chestertown merchants and grandees. A Scottish factor in Oxford, Talbot County, noted that if such a boycott had happened, they would want for English items such as "nails, without which they cannot build or repair their houses; hoes, without which they cannot cultivate their Tobacco or Indian Corn; and course cloths, without this article they must perish as the winter is exceedingly cold here." Nonimportation was not accepted on the trade-dependent Eastern Shore.

FIRST CONVENTION

Initially, Maryland was governed by a newly created Assembly of Freemen, which was a provincial convention. The first convention was held from June 22 to June 25, 1774. All sixteen existing counties were represented by a total of ninety-two members, although voting was by each county, not individual members. Thomas Smyth was named Kent County's representative, and Talbot County's Matthew Tilghman was elected chairman.

ASSOCIATION OF THE FREEMEN OF MARYLAND

After hostilities broke out at Lexington and Concord, the Association of the Freemen of Maryland was formed in Annapolis on July 26, 1775, by the county delegates to the provincial convention. Among the 141 delegates, Kent County's were William Ringgold Jr., Colonel Richard Lloyd, Thomas Smyth, Joseph Earle and Thomas Bedingfield Hands. Matthew Tilghman was again chosen as a chairman.

The members of the association contended that the "now avowed design of the British Government, to raise a revenue from the property of the colonists without their consent [and] the arbitrary and vindictive statutes passed against…Massachusetts Bay…are sufficient causes to arm a free people in defense of their liberty, and to justify resistance." As inhabitants of Maryland, they were firmly persuaded that it was necessary to repel force by force and "do approve of the opposition by arms to the British troops." Furthermore, they pledged to do "the utmost of our power, to promote and support the present opposition, carrying on, as well by arms, as by the continental association, restraining our commerce." Thus, this group supported war for the first time.

While the association members were willing to arm, they still held out an olive branch of reconciliation and dissociated themselves from rash acts of violence. They were at pains to reassure that "in these times of public danger…a reconciliation with Great Britain is an event we most ardently wish may soon take place." They admitted that they were on a path toward anarchy but claimed to "solemnly engage in maintenance of good order, and the public peace, to support the civil power in the due execution of the laws…and to defend with our utmost power all persons from every species of outrage to themselves or their property, and to prevent any punishment, from being inflicted on any offenders." Thus, while Maryland should go to war and aid Massachusetts, members were still open to constitutional reconciliation and would do their utmost to prevent anarchy. These sentiments, which were as radical as it would get, evidently had the support of the Eastern Shore delegates.

CHESTERTOWN PARTICIPATES

Throughout the late 1760s and early 1770s, the Royal Navy stepped up its activities to collect duties and prevent smuggling. Schooners like the Boston-built *Sultana* were purchased in 1768 to serve as coast guard vessels. The *Sultana*'s duties included stints in the lower Chesapeake Bay and Delaware, although it never docked at Chestertown. It was retired in 1772 and sold a year later in England, as the Royal Navy required larger and better-armed patrol craft. A replica of the *Sultana* was launched in Chestertown in 2001 and today provides educational sailing excursions.

In 1766, the Sons of Liberty organized themselves in Kent County to seek repeal of the Stamp Act, which they regarded as a tax forced upon them by Parliament without the consent of their assembly. The names of attendees at this earliest gathering would become familiar in the movement for independence: two Thomas Ringgolds (father and son), William Ringgold, Thomas Smythe, William Bordley, two Joseph Nicholsons (father

A 2001 replica of the Royal Navy ship *Sultana*. An eight-gun schooner, it served in American waters to collect duties and prevent smuggling from 1768 to 1772.

and son) and Peroy Frisby. However, the Stamp Act was quickly repealed, and Chestertown remained quiet for the next eight years.

Not until 1774 were merchant pocketbooks again affected by the Parliament's acts. A local source of friction did exist. Merchants felt that the Chestertown's customs collector and fellow merchant, William Geddes, was using his position to line his pockets, failing to pay the duties he levied on others. Geddes had left his home in Princess Anne County in 1755 and must have served as Chestertown's customs collector after 1763, before his reappointment in 1767. Among other enterprises, he purchased a lot on Church Alley and built a modest house, separate from the customhouse. Regardless of the conflict of interest, he obtained a franchise from the West India Trade Company, which he ran in partnership with Chestertown sailors. He claimed his customs salary was not sufficient to support his family. In 1770, this claim was confirmed by an inspector general, who suggested that Geddes's salary be paid out of public treasury, not from the proceeds of the office. The inspector also ordered Geddes to give up his franchise, as it was an obvious conflict of interest and created a temptation to smuggle.

Geddes did not do what the inspector recommended. This was proved by the May 7, 1774 arrival of the brigantine *Geddes* at Chestertown after having passed through customs at Annapolis with a load of London goods. It is not clear what the cargo consisted of, but certainly there must have been some tea and, possibly, spices, silk and Chinese ceramics. The ship's cargo did not belong to the infamous East India Company, whose failure had caused Parliament to send tea to the colonies, but rather to another Chestertown merchant, James Nicholson, who would sign the Tea Resolves produced during the *Geddes*'s visit.

On May 13, 1774, in reaction to the *Geddes*'s arrival and inspired by the earlier Boston Tea Party and the resulting closure of the port of Boston, citizens of Chestertown met to discuss the situation. They were aware that cargo with dutiable tea was on the locally built *Geddes* and that Nicholson was the owner of the cargo. They met again on the twenty-fourth and approved a newly written set of resolves that prohibited the buying, selling or drinking of tea. They acknowledged George III as their sovereign, "to whom we owe and promise all dutiful allegiance and submission." Still, "no duties or taxes can constitutionally be imposed on us, but by our own consent, given personally, or by our representatives." They then argued that Parliament's duty on tea to raise revenue was unconstitutional and "calculated to enslave Americans." Another resolution contended that any citizen found importing or purchasing dutiable tea would be stigmatized as an enemy of American liberties. This resolution may have been aimed directly at Geddes. However, he remained in Chestertown and was still acting as a merchant there in 1782.

No violence or destruction of property was involved. The *Geddes* left Chestertown on May 24, the day the resolves were approved, bound for Madeira with a cargo of wheat and flour, evidently its business successfully completed. Still, the group that drafted the resolves would continue to meet and, on June 2, would become the Kent County Committee of Correspondence.

This Chestertown committee proposed to collect a subscription for the poor of Boston, whose port has been closed. Some merchants agreed to share the cost of sending Captain John Wethered to Boston with a cargo of Kent County's flour. The subscribers included Emory Sudler and James Nicholson. The flour arrived in Boston in June or July 1774, and Samuel Adams thanked them with the words, "We cannot but applaud the spirit and determined virtue of the Town of Chester." Thus, Chestertown's merchants joined those from throughout the colonies in shipping flour to Boston.

In an altercation beyond Chestertown in the Sassafras-Bohemia area in March 1775, the surveyor of the area seized two wagons of goods being carried toward Delaware's Duck Creek without having paid duties. However, the officer was overpowered by a "licentious mob" shouting, "Liberty and Duck Creek forever!" The Crown official was tarred and feathered, a ritual that endangered his life.

FORMING COMMITTEES

In September 1775, a Scottish factor reported from Talbot County that civil government had been ended, and in its place had been "substituted Congresses, Conventions, Committees and Mobs, who put their laws in execution with a high hand." The movement for independence was promoted by such gatherings.

In Kent County, committees would be revived in 1774 as a result of the resolves and play critical roles in ending local British government by providing direction before the colonial legislatures and Congress. Committee members were usually appointed by leading rebels rather than elected. By April 1775, Congress gave them the authority to enforce and administer the pledge of support to the nonimportation association. Committee members also received authorization to search for, publicize and condemn those who refused to acknowledge the authority of Congress. Nonsigners and nonjurors were to be exposed to public scorn, to have their interests discredited and to be ostracized. The purpose was to prevent an opposition to the Congress from forming.

Congress failed to describe the means of carrying out these activities, and no effort was made to have the committees operate as legal entities. While they used the threat of tarring and feathering, placing their victims on rails and even hanging, they usually favored persuasion. Many people were forced to disclaim the king and his government, but the oaths given were worthless since they were obtained under obvious duress. The committees attempted to prevent Loyalists from forming military units and joining the war. Rebel militia under their command was ordered to carry out a watchful policy of house visits, under the cover of darkness, to undermine Loyalists' efforts to organize or to reach the safety of the British military.

Established during the *Geddes* crisis, the Kent County Committee of Correspondence held its first formal meeting at the Chestertown Courthouse and then held future meetings at Edward Worrell's tavern at the corner of Cannon and Queen Streets. The chair was Thomas Smyth, and William Hall served as clerk. Notable committeemen included two William Ringgolds, John Maxwell, Emory Sudler, attorney Joseph Earle, Colonel Richard Lloyd, John Cadwalader, James Hynson, Donaldson Yeates, Colonel Joseph Nicholson, Joseph Nicholson Jr. and Captain James Nicholson. They aimed to end local British government and prevent the development of Loyalism.

Additionally, the Eastern Shore had a branch of the Maryland Council of Safety at Chestertown, which met beginning in 1775. The assembly had established the Council of Safety in August 1775 with sixteen members, half of them nominated from the Eastern Shore. The council had the authority to draw funds, summon conventions and call out troops. When it first met in 1775, Richard and Edward Lloyd and Thomas Smyth were council members. In practice, the Eastern Shore and Western Committees often met separately. Smyth continued to serve in most subsequent meetings, which later saw the additions of Joseph Nicholson Jr. and Thomas Bedingfield Hands. However, in January 1776, the assembly swept all of this away. The new Council of Safety had two committees, one for recruiting and sustaining troops and the other to regulate them. The seven-member council had only three members from the Eastern Shore, the Western Shore having the majority. The new council acted as a court that could pardon death penalties or banish the disaffected from Maryland. It came to an end in March 1777. Doubtless some members of these councils were upset by the assembly's constant revision of the committees' authority.

A Committees of Observation replaced the ad-hoc Committees of Correspondence that early on had led the protest against Parliament and sometimes had become too zealous. The Committees of Safety sought to restrict the membership of local Committees of Observation to men of substance. The Kent County Committee of Observation controlled munitions and issued supply contracts. In June 1776, for instance, it delivered the public powder lodged in Mr. Slubey's Chestertown warehouse to Joseph Middleton. It appears that these county committees also took over many of the duties of the British court system.

Chestertown became one of the most important places on the Eastern Shore for the accumulation of munitions and firearms. In June 1776, Chestertown's Elisha Winters, a large manufacturer of firearms, was designated by the Committee of Safety as the official gunsmith for the Eastern Shore. Later in the war, an Eastern Shore Treasury existed and was often raided for needed funds by the state treasury in Annapolis.

DECLINE OF THE ROYAL GOVERNOR

Maryland royal governor Robert Eden had an effective kinship network, and he remained popular and was respected in the Maryland legislature. Eden was a descendant of a prominent Irish family, as his father and grandfather had both served in Parliament. He received an officer's commission; married Caroline Calvert, daughter of the fifth Lord Baltimore; and came to Maryland in 1769 with a governor's commission in hand. As late as 1774, the legislature created Caroline County from parts of Dorchester and Queen Anne's Counties on the Eastern Shore, honoring Eden's wife, Lady Caroline.

Eden was a good governor, opposing the taxing efforts of the Crown's ministry but also drawing the line at talk of independence. Meanwhile, Congress saw royal governors as the enemy, and it attempted to topple them by using its new Continental army. Impatient in 1776, Major General Charles Lee and Congress ordered the Baltimore Committee of Observation to "get rid of [Eden's] damn'd Government." However, the Maryland Committee of Safety felt it had been subverted and refused to arrest the governor. The committee was made up of Maryland's rebel leaders: no fewer than two Carrolls, William Paca, Samuel Chase, Thomas Johnson and Chestertown's Thomas Smyth. No one could tell them how to handle Maryland's governor. Effort was made in Baltimore to discredit the Committee of Safety, showing fresh division in the rebel cause. Lord Dunmore eventually rescued Eden by sending the HMS *Fowey* from his fleet on Chesapeake Bay, and on June 26, 1776, Eden and his supporters left Annapolis on board this vessel.

CONTROVERSIAL NEW CONSTITUTION

While the committees were functioning in Chestertown, a new state government was being produced in Annapolis. After Eden left, the state of Maryland was run by impermanent provincial conventions until the middle of 1776. The first representatives from Kent County in 1774 were from the old families: Thomas Smyth, William and Thomas Ringgold, Joseph Nicholson Jr., Joseph Earle and William Hall. Most continued to be reelected to further conventions. In fact, the Ringgolds had continuously represented Kent County at Annapolis since the 1760s.

By the eighth convention, it was decided that the continuation of the ad-hoc government was not in step with the more radical colonies. Maryland congressmen Samuel Chase and Charles Carroll of Carrollton wanted a more permanent and structured government that answered Congress's call to the states to form new governments. On July 3, 1776, the convention resolved to elect a new convention that would be responsible for drawing up their first state constitution. On August 1, freemen who could meet existing property qualifications of the provincial legislature were elected delegates to the ninth constitution-making convention. It would be the last convention, as the delegates would draft a constitution.

However, before this convention met, the process of selecting its delegates was challenged by five counties, three of them on the Eastern Shore: Kent, Queen Anne's and Worcester. Kent County's convention franchise was very restrictive—so much so that out of 3,500 free whites, only 74 were eligible to vote. As for standing for an office, in Kent County, less than 14 percent of the free white males were eligible to serve in the Lower House, and only about 9 percent were eligible to serve in the Upper House. This explained why a few families of grandees had monopolized political representation for decades.

On election day in the Eastern Shore counties, the property qualifications that had prevented most of the inhabitants from voting were ignored, and the franchise was extended to all tax payers who bore arms. This was a protest, as Kent County's election judges—William Rogers, William Bordley and John Page—were forcibly thrown out. It was a bid to expand the franchise that Congressman Samuel Chase feared, and when the elected delegates were convened in Annapolis, the representatives of the three Eastern Shore counties were disqualified and new elections were ordered. This time, the property qualifications were enforced, but the newly elected delegates from Kent County were nearly the same: Thomas and William Ringgold, Joseph Earle, Colonel Richard Lloyd and Thomas Smyth. Chase had been unable to change the representation of Kent and the other Eastern Shore counties.

Thus, Kent County's leadership expressed resentment against the colonial legislature and the Annapolis grandee leadership that had continued to dominate the conventions. Their protest also supported the idea that those who served in the military deserved recognition for risking their lives and thus should be allowed to vote despite the fact they could not qualify for the franchise.

The new constitution was the document by which Maryland was governed from 1777 into the nineteenth century. It contained no balance of powers such as those found in the English Constitution. Molded by the grandees, it made no attempt to create a more democratic society, holding to restriction of the franchise and voting procedures so that the planters and merchants would continue to control politics. Senators in the Upper House were not even directly elected by voters; rather, chosen electors gathered at Annapolis to pick the senators from those assembled or the general population. Continued high property-holding qualifications restricted government offices. Rotation of office, rather than popular election, was favored so that governors were selected annually by the legislature. This limited their power because their terms were further restricted to no more than three years in succession out of seven. It was argued that the governors and senators had to be men of wealth, high birth and ability so that they could not be corrupted. They were expected to stand against unreasonable popular pressures from below and prevent anarchy. Maryland's new government perpetuated rule by men of wealth and property, but this was not supported in Kent County.

KENT COUNTY'S GRANDEES ARE REPLACED

Kent County's representatives to the new assembly were Peregrine Letherbury, Isaac Perkins, John Maxwell and Donaldson Yeates. Letherbury was a newcomer who would support the future creation of Washington College, while Maxwell was a landowner involved in the effort to establish a Presbyterian church in Georgetown. The selection of Perkins and Yeates made more sense. It has been seen that Isaac Perkins was from a middling Kent County family. Born in 1743, he owned White House Farm along with his brother Thomas, but he also lived on nearby Muddy Branch Farm, established in 1774. While he served as a soldier in New York in 1776, he retired from combat and profited by supplying both Continental and Maryland soldiers. A Maryland Convention named him colonel of militia but assigned him to the Procurement Office, making him a purchasing agent for the Continental army. He had also led the mob that, early in 1777, attacked James Chalmers when he returned to Chestertown.

Donaldson Yeates, originally a merchant from New Castle, Delaware, came to Kent County in the 1760s. With a partner, he purchased seven acres from Henry Knox, called Knox's Folly. This Turner's Creek farm consisted of a granary on the wharf and a modest log house, built about 1760. Yeates expanded the house with a brick addition and rented it to his nephew John Lathim, who became his business partner and handled many of his affairs.

Yeates continued to add to his land holdings, and by 1783, he had fifty-six slaves and sixty white tenants living at Turner's Creek.

Both Perkins and Yeates were self-made men of middle rank, who owed their success to productive farms and their ability to obtain military contracts, without the need for a presence in Chestertown society. Their political careers continued, and they would eventually represent Kent County at the convention to ratify the federal constitution in 1788. Thus, none of the four Kent County representatives were from the grandee leadership that had participated in the conventions and the drafting of the new constitution. Thomas Smyth, William Ringgold and Richard Lloyd would never again serve in the legislature. We can only surmise that they felt the new constitution was flawed.

New Government Fails on the Eastern Shore

The new government confronted various problems on the Eastern Shore that were not directly related to the independence movement. The representative election process that had already been questioned by some Eastern Shore counties broke down in the southernmost county of Somerset. When the new legislature convened in February 1777 for its first meeting, no representatives from Somerset County appeared. It was explained that shortly after the polls had opened, the authorities were confronted by rioters from all over the county, carrying firearms fixed with sticks and spears at end of them. The mob closed the polls, preventing the election. The new legislature responded by authorizing two thousand troops to the Eastern Shore to suppress "that dangerous insurrection." Intelligence also came from Congress that the British had planned "an expedition to [Chesapeake Bay] in the ensuing campaign and that the Eastern Shore is the first objective or place of landing." Thus, the new rebel government responded to election discord with unrealistic attempts at subduing the rioters by force.

Salt Riots

In another October 1776 incident, riots to obtain salt occurred in the middle counties of Talbot and Dorchester, when it was time for ordinary families to salt their meat for the winter. The salt riots were inspired by the lack of its availability to the lower orders and the lack of old-fashioned landlord paternalism, which had disappeared as the gentry became capitalistic. Salt was important to the Eastern Shore diet and economy as a preservative. During the war, the curtailment of trade with Europe prevented salt from reaching the region, and its shortage caused high prices for what did get through. The Committee of Observation in Dorchester County reported that "the want for the absolute necessities of life is so great that many families for months past have not had a spoonful of salt." The salt protesters were class conscious, expressing anger at the engrossing and market exploitation of wealthy rebel planters, who sought to monopolize the supply and raise the price of salt—a traditional complaint of crowds in both England and its colonies. Some rebel leaders, like James Lloyd Chamberlaine, felt so victimized when state authorities turned a deaf ear to his complaints about the rioters stealing his salt that he gave up his positions in the military and government.

Old Kent County Families Waiver

Against such a background of discord and anarchy, the Maryland government sought firm supporters. Matthew Tilghman of Talbot County was one of the Eastern Shore leading grandees and a devotee of the Revolutionary cause that was orchestrated from Annapolis. He was an early member of Maryland's Committee of Correspondence and became chairman of the state Committee of Safety, president of the Revolutionary assembly and the head of the Maryland delegation to the Continental Congress. He voted for the final approval of the Declaration of Independence, but Annapolis grandees replaced him with Charles Carroll of Carrollton, who was sent before a copy could be signed.

Tilghman was named president over a session of the Annapolis Convention that established Maryland's new constitution. It is not clear as to where he stood on the issue of a wider electorate, but Talbot County was for it. When the new state government went into effect in late 1776, Tilghman was elected to the Senate, where he would serve until 1783. He quickly retired from public life when the war was over. Here was a paragon of Revolutionary virtue that would be difficult to match anywhere on the Eastern Shore.

In contrast, we have a more mixed picture with the grandees of Kent. True, William Ringgold and Thomas Smyth showed themselves to be rebels, but their support stopped short of government service after the new constitution went into effect. The grandees of Kent seemed only mildly interested in the rebel cause. William Ringgold, the brother and partner of Thomas V, became the leader of the family just as the Revolution was breaking out. He had expected his brother to continue in politics, but his brother's untimely death had shocked him, and he may have been unprepared for the weighty duties that fell on his shoulders. William represented the family by serving on the Maryland Committee of Safety, and in 1776, he was a member of the convention that drew up Maryland's new constitution. He received a militia commission from the highly regarded Mathew Tilghman. But this is the extent of his Revolutionary career.

No one among Kent County's rebels was more important than Thomas Smyth III. It has been noted that he was descended from an old family. Smyth and his business partner and brother-in-law, Emory Sudler, owned the schooner *Friendship* and shipped wheat to Spain and Portugal. Smyth held thirty-five slaves in 1790, making him the sixth-largest slave owner in the county, and Sudler owned eleven. In addition to his plantations, Smyth also operated a mercantile business from his Chestertown home, Widehall, near the foot of High Street.

Smyth was a justice of the Kent County Court during the peaceful and prosperous 1760s. He also represented Kent County at the Provincial Conventions and, in 1770, was a member of a committee set up to investigate the increase of taxation on English imports. In 1776, he signed the Association of Freemen of Maryland. From 1774 to 1776, Smyth was a member of the

An 1802 sketch of Thomas Smyth III. Smyth was a grandee and leading rebel in the early years of the Revolution. *Kent County Historical Society.*

Maryland Committee of Safety, in charge of providing munitions, meat and flour for the troops enlisted in Kent. He was a co-owner of the Chestertown ropewalk and was able to build two galleys for the navy at his shipyard. While a good record, it showed political ambivalence after 1776 and thus came no where near Tilghman's service to the Annapolis government.

While Thomas Smyth left politics, in a sense, he was replaced by his twenty-year-old son, Thomas Smyth IV. Along with Isaac Perkins, Thomas Jr. was the other captain of a company of volunteers that went to the Flying Camp to serve as a reserve for the Continental army. His father did all he could to supply and equip the companies as the son led his men to New York. Still, by 1779, Thomas Jr. was out of the army, using his law training as a Kent County justice of peace and a judge of Orphans' Court.

Perhaps the Kent County grandees were aging. While Richard Lloyd had served as a militia colonel during the colonial wars, when the independence movement came, he decided to limit his activities to politics. In June 1774, Richard was a member of the Kent County Committee of Correspondence. A year later, he was sent to represent Kent County on the first Maryland Council of Safety. In April and July 1775, Richard, along with Thomas Smyth, William and Thomas Ringgold and Joseph Nicholson Jr., was a delegate to the fourth and fifth conventions of Maryland government. However, Richard then dropped out of politics and never again represented Kent County. To an extent, this was absolved by the fact that his son James Lloyd was elected in 1777–78 and 1782 to the Maryland Assembly and also served as a lieutenant in the Kent County militia. The younger generation was now more willing to go to Annapolis.

Prior to the war, the Hynsons had served as Kent County's representatives to the Provincial Assembly, but they did not hold political office during the War for Independence. Charles Carvill Hynson of Bungay Hill became a Methodist and would not bear arms. William, Nathaniel, Charles and James Hynson did serve as privates in the militia. Cornelius, Edward and William Comegys also served as privates in the militia. One must assume that these were younger sons or from lesser branches of the families. As for the Carvills, we know only that John was a pew holder in Chester Parish church in 1772. Such was the mundane role of some of the old families during the War for Independence.

The exception among the grandee families was William Bordley, son of John Beal Bordley, who had provided his sons with farms in Kent County. As a younger son, in 1774, William had supported the sending of flour to the poor of Boston. But two years later, he had been overruled as election judge protecting the narrow franchise's status quo. In 1777, he was in charge of raising militia to be sent to Somerset County to quell the insurrection. A year later, he worked with Smallwood to catch the notorious Loyalist Cheney Clow, calling him dangerous and still at large in the swamps, where scouting parties must be sent to confine him. Bordley became colonel of the Thirteenth Battalion of Kent County militia in 1778 and 1779. A year later, he would offer to provide defense for his and his father's Wye River plantations using Kent County militia.

In sum, after delay, Kent County leaders would join the movement for independence, writing Tea Resolves and providing grain for the poor in the closed port of Boston. Representatives went to Annapolis to serve in the convention government that gave way to the Constitution of 1776, which failed to broaden the franchise. Kent County had its own Committee of Correspondence as result of the Tea Resolves, followed by a state-sponsored Committee of Observation. The Annapolis government lost control of much of the Eastern Shore, initially because of election disorders and the class-conscious salt riots. A situation developed in which the Annapolis government could not depend on the leaders of Kent County or the Eastern Shore. As the war progressed, the Kent County grandees found they could offer only temperate support for the new government established by the Constitution of 1776.

Chapter 7

Going to War: A Variety of Choices

During the Revolution, no formal battles were fought or land invasions conducted on the Eastern Shore. Yet conflict was constant throughout the war, as a civil war raged, causing deep divisions within society.

Many on the Eastern Shore had gained military experience in the Seven Years' War as militia, volunteers or ships' officers. In 1755, when hostilities broke out against the French, thirty Kent County militia were easily raised without the benefit of a recruitment drum. A year later, Chestertown gentry fitted out a ship, the *Sharpe*, named for the governor. It carried twenty-six guns and twenty swivels and was manned by crew of two hundred. It was the first of several privateers that were soon causing havoc among French and Spanish ships.

MILITIA

The militia raised by colonial legislatures during the colonial wars against France consisted mostly of men between the ages of sixteen and sixty, who were required to provide their own arms and ammunition and muster on designated days. From this legislation, in 1775, the Maryland Convention allowed militia companies the option of electing their own officers, just as they did in New England. A year later, the assembly authorized seventeen battalions of militia on the Eastern Shore, with James Lloyd Chamberlaine (the victim of the salt riots) serving as brigadier for the upper counties, including Kent. Each county would be responsible for organizing and outfitting militia companies to protect against invasion and to support the Continental army. The ranks of these militiamen contained many undecided citizens who would eventually become Loyalists. They simply were obeying the law of universal conscription, which they would ignore by not showing up or by showing up in such force that the militia was dispersed. They were not sought after, as finding them caused more difficulty than they were worth. To maximize the number of men who might serve, the Maryland government was most liberal—especially for a southern state—in that it allowed recruits who were normally forbidden. Indentured servants were not required to obtain the consent of their masters, and vagrants and felons were offered pardons for satisfactory military service. Under certain conditions, even slaves could be recruited.

Over the entire war, the Kent muster rolls bear the names of about 1,500 men who volunteered for militia or special service. These volunteers comprised the Thirteenth Battalion of militia, commanded by Colonel Richard Graves, and the Twenty-seventh Battalion, under Colonel Donaldson Yeates. The quality of the troops, with the exception of the Continentals, was always in question. It was not exactly their fault, for often the militia had no arms, ammunition or clothing necessary for service. Furthermore, when Kent County militia found no enemy to contend with or was routed, they deserted in droves, and reenlistment possibilities disappeared. Many militiamen integrated their service into their family obligations and work routine so that at harvest time, they were always absent.

SPECIAL UNITS

Other units were created early in the war because the militia could not respond quickly, was often ill equipped and was thinned of its best men, who were put to better use in these units. These units included independent companies, Minutemen and the reserve of the Flying Camp.

INDEPENDENT COMPANIES

Independent companies were unique in makeup and were regarded as superior to the ordinary militia company. They were usually formed from the militia but with their own uniforms and equipment, which each man could afford. Often, they formed units of light infantry and cavalry. In 1776, Kent County's Thomas Smyth Jr. was captain of such an elite company of light infantry. Most famous of these companies in 1775 was that of Mordecai Gist, a future Continental general, who gathered the young men of Baltimore's best families together under the title of the Baltimore Independent Company. It was the first volunteer rebel company raised in Maryland, and Gist was elected captain and paraded them in their brilliant red uniforms. Gist's company would be integrated in Maryland's Continental regiments. Because the companies owed their allegiance to their founder or a political club that covered their initial expenses rather than a state or Congress, they acted independently of the rest of the militia. Groups of company commanders could follow their own convictions rather than those of a commanding general. The captains were even accused of telling their men how to vote in elections. Also in this category were bands of volunteers for hire. After the Wye Valley plantations in Talbot County were devastated by the enemy in March 1781, forty-seven wealthy area rebels took matters into their own hands and collectively paid for the recruitment and operating costs of officers and twenty men to protect them by patrolling in the barge *Experiment*.

MINUTEMEN

Realizing that the militia was slow to mobilize and that the independent companies could be temperamental, the Maryland Convention created companies of Minutemen, copying the example of those created earlier in Massachusetts. Theoretically, they were the best of the militia as they had arms, ammunition and clothing within their household and thus could be called upon at minute's notice for an immediate crisis. The reality of these expectations was never realized, and the creation of Minutemen in Maryland was abandoned on March 1, 1776.

When the call for Minutemen was issued in January 1776, Kent County furnished a company consisting of four officers, four sergeants, four corporals, one surgeon, one fifer, one drummer and seventy men "fit for duty." Captain

William Henry was in command, and his troops were to assist Virginia troops in repelling a threatened British invasion. They marched from Chestertown in late January, their destination being Northampton Court House, Virginia, where they arrived on February 12, the first Minutemen to reach Northampton. The Queen Anne's County company under Captain James Kent arrived two days later. Evidently, the Minutemen had moved quickly, fulfilling the expectations embodied in their name.

However, the reason for discontinuing the Minutemen is evident in the failure of the Kent and Queen Anne's Minutemen that followed. The Maryland Convention called on them for a rapid foray against the insurrection on the lower Eastern Shore. Kent County's contingent consisted of eighty-six men under Captain William Henry who were joined with a company of Queen Anne's Minutemen. Henry's company had already been serving in Northampton County, Virginia, and came back to Chestertown. On February 3, 1776, the Minutemen began to march southward toward Snow Hill in Worcester County. They lacked provisions, and many were reported as marching barefoot in the icy winter weather. It took almost a month for them to cover the one-hundred-mile distance, and by the time they arrived, their enlistments were due to expire. They soon turned around and went home. The insurrection in Worcester County continued, but the raising of Minutemen in Maryland would be discontinued.

FLYING CAMP

In March 1776, faced with defending an expansive territory in the Middle Colonies from British operations, Washington recommended the formation of a "flying camp," which he referred to as "a mobile, strategic reserve of troops." Congress agreed and on June 3, 1776, passed a resolution "that a flying camp be immediately established in the Middle Colonies and that it consist of 10,000 men." Militiamen were recruited from three colonies—6,000 from Pennsylvania, 3,400 from Maryland and 600 from Delaware—and were to serve until December 1, 1776. They were to be paid and fed in the same manner as Continentals. Two companies were to be raised in Kent County, and on July 6, the Maryland Assembly commissioned Isaac Perkins as captain of a Kent County company that went to the Flying Camp at Amboy, New Jersey. Joseph Earle was named lieutenant colonel, but by mid-August, he had been replaced, and it is unlikely that he went with the unit. As foreseen, the militia would stay only for a month rather than until the end of the year, so the camp experienced high desertion rates and even munity on the part of the politicized Philadelphia militia. The Flying Camp disappeared at the end of the year, although the remaining units served at the Battles of Long Island and White Plains.

COPING WITH THE EASTERN SHORE MILITIA

In 1777, Maryland state leader William Paca, en route to Congress in Philadelphia from his plantation in Queen Anne's County, was stranded in Chestertown. While in the town, he observed that the militia was deficient in experienced officers, arms and ammunition. At least three hundred militiamen had been sent home because of lack of muskets. What follows is a litany of the difficulties of raising men for the rebel cause in Kent County and, for that matter, everywhere on the Eastern Shore.

Paca's analysis shows why recruiting for military service on the Eastern Shore was difficult. While the militia became an organization controlled by the Maryland government, in practice, militia companies were often more loyal to their commanding captain than any other authority—thus, if the captain favored the Crown, his men did as well. In September 1775, the company of Captain George Day Scott was mustering on the Wicomico River in Somerset County to enlist recruits and choose officers. For militia service, a collection of fishermen and farmers were formed on the road, but another group, with red cockades rather than the rebel's black in their hats, formed on the opposite side. They were commanded by Sergeant Isaac Atkinson. He told his men to bring sharp flints to the muster, a sign that they were ready for hostilities. Atkinson threatened that his men would fire their weapons as a salute to break up the company. When confronted by Scott, Atkinson asserted that he could recruit hundreds of men to join in opposition to the state council. His men supported him as "the man who ought to be upheld." Atkinson's company remained separate.

Scott had to get back at Atkinson for humiliating him, thus he had him brought before the Somerset County Committee of Observation. In the courthouse, all the hearsay Scott could muster was used against Atkinson. But Atkinson denied the charges, and fifty of his followers, armed with short clubs, waited outside the courthouse. The committee was overawed by the force, so it let Atkinson go. Atkinson told them, "A day must be appointed, and they must fight it out." Mustering showed the divisions within the militia, which weakened the rebel cause. With no procedures, Committees of Observation usually bowed to the popular side.

Outside guidance from an authority like the Annapolis Committee of Safety was not appreciated on the Eastern Shore. When Thomas Sparrow was sent to Dorchester County with a commission to raise a force of artillerymen to protect Annapolis, his duty took him to a county chapel (probably Anglican Trinity Church), where he began to read the recruitment order. Suddenly, a person in the audience challenged him, stating that the men he was recruiting would not be sent to Annapolis but rather Philadelphia, where they would have to fight against their king in defense of the city. Sparrow was then approached by several men, who struck his notice and threatened that if he did not flee, he would be murdered. He escaped and was followed, but he took to the woods and survived, albeit without help from the cowardly Dorchester County Committee of Observation.

These incidents were further complicated by the issue of appointing or electing officers, which you will remember had been made an option. Colonel Thomas Wright of Queen Anne's County reported that his appointed militia officers were being ignored because militiamen favored electing their own militia officers. Since Wright himself was appointed, he could not find a solution to the dilemma of choosing officers. The problem received a solution not from the Committee of Safety in Annapolis but rather Maryland's representatives in Congress. When a Worcester County officer complained to the congressional delegation in Philadelphia, it recommended that unpopular officers be removed and replaced by those acceptable to the troops. Disciplined militia officers thus became candidates for removal among the easygoing militia. Clearly, such a procedure undermined the ability of officers to command, and many units ended up without a commanding officer. Furthermore, the appeal to the congressional delegation undermined the authority of the Maryland Committee of Safety.

In the early years, no funds existed for rebel recruiting. Later in the war, however, the recruiting system became better financed. By 1780, Kent County militia officers, like Captain Edward Wright of the Seventh Regiment and Ensign John Sears of the Second Regiment, were paid for recruiting by the tax collector for Kent County. The same authority also paid for the necessities of the collected recruits while they stayed in Chestertown.

Continued Eastern Shore Insurrection

At the beginning of 1777, the Maryland Council of Safety asked Congress for help because it simply did not have the resources to break the Eastern Shore insurrection. The council had attempted to put together a militia force under Brigadier General Hooper, but it had failed, as the troops were not sufficient enough to quell the uprisings. Congress responded by sending two Continental officers, William Smallwood and Mordecai Gist, along with a few Continentals, to quell the Eastern Shore rebellion. To further advance the effort, political commissioners accompanied the soldiers to enforce the decrees of the new government and Congress. In choosing the two officers, Congress was simply ratifying the Maryland government's concern that the commanders be Marylanders.

The commander of Maryland's first Continental regiment, Brigadier General William Smallwood, seemed ideal for the job of ending the insurrection, and he was able to ferry his Continentals across Chesapeake Bay and into the affected area. Smallwood was to become Maryland's leading military commander, famous as a drillmaster. Born in 1732 on the Western Shore, his father, a merchant-planter, sent him to Britain for his education. He served in the Seven Years' War and, after his return, was elected to the Lower House of the General Assembly. He subscribed to the Maryland Nonimportation Association in 1769, was a delegate to the Maryland Convention of 1775 and signed the Association of Freemen of Maryland. However, he was slow to support independence. His connections to the legislators in the new government at Annapolis made him a popular choice.

Smallwood brought with him a February 1777 proclamation from the Maryland Assembly that claimed the inhabitants of Somerset and Worcester Counties had collected "an armed force, and by erecting the standard of the king of Great Britain have invited the…enemy into their country." This opposition had to be crushed, and the assembly instructed Smallwood that the inhabitants of the two counties be gathered in places he directed, give up their arms and take an oath of allegiance to the state government. Upon strict compliance, a full pardon was offered, and grievances were to be speedily redressed. Excluded from the process were fourteen ringleaders.

FAILURE

At first, Smallwood reported that all was quiet on the Eastern Shore, and he dismissed most of his troops in March. However, within a few weeks, he found that his authority was openly flouted. He complained, "What have you to expect from those who have cut down liberty poles, and in direct opposition thereto, have erected the king's standard, and in an avowed manner drunk his health and success, and destruction to Congress and conventions?" Smallwood soon left, and his command fell upon Gist, with his few Continentals. A total of only 287 people in the counties had complied with the assembly's proclamation.

In Worcester County, Joseph Dashiell, the lord lieutenant, found that the assembly's proclamation was ignored for three reasons: some were sick, others wished to remain home and support neither side and still others were obstinately attached to the old form of government. The last group was identified by aristocratic Dashiell as the poor and contemptible. "Despicable as those creatures...are," he explained, "they have their influence within their own peculiar sphere." Certainly, he was referring to the lower sort.

The other Continental officer in charge of the Eastern Shore pacification was Colonel Mordecai Gist. Born in 1742 in Baltimore into the prominent Cockey family, Gist was a third cousin of George Washington. After raising the Baltimore Independent Company, he joined William Smallwood's Continental battalion as a major, although he yearned for actual combat rather than administrative duties. He was involved in the attempted arrest of Governor Robert Eden, which the legislature quashed. Gist went on to serve with Washington when Sir William Howe conquered New York. After Washington's Trenton victory, Colonel Gist was allowed to return to Maryland to assist in rebuilding his ranks, which had fallen from 750 to 300. He and Smallwood considered recruiting Continentals and procuring supplies as more important than putting down the continuous Eastern Shore insurrection. They were becoming aware that Continentals were not effective in quelling local insurrection. Gist doggedly recruited in the upper Eastern Shore counties, writing off Somerset and Worcester Counties because of their discontent. By July, he had succeeded in sending 200 new Continental recruits to the main army, including some from Kent County.

Maryland Militia in Pennsylvania

As Sir William Howe invaded Chesapeake Bay at the beginning of September 1777, Congress issued a call for the Maryland, Pennsylvania and Delaware militias to support the Continental army. The response of most of the Middle Colonies was to place their militia under the Continental army. Maryland claimed exclusive jurisdiction over its troops, refusing to place them in the Continental command and instead choosing William Smallwood as militia commander. Colonel Gist was to continue raising militia on the Eastern Shore and then lead them to Washington's army. Having already experienced the Eastern Shore insurrection, Smallwood and Gist wondered where the militia would get its arms, food, clothing, ammunition, officers and organization.

Defending Philadelphia, Washington decided he needed Maryland militia reinforcements to harass the rear of Howe's army and block him while his overworked Continentals sought to intercept Howe. Washington realized that few militia were available because they were already stationed on the shore of the Chesapeake to prevent "negros and stock being swept away" by the British fleet. Moreover, harvest time was also coming, an ideal excuse to go home. Washington also pinpointed the past lack of good militia officers, stating, "Without some leaders to form and command them…a greater part will disband."

Plagued by a lack of equipment and officers, as commissions had not been issued in the upper Eastern Shore, Gist was unable to meet Washington's initial order to gather militia at Georgetown and move toward Delaware and Pennsylvania until September 10. By then, Howe had decisively defeated Washington at Brandywine. Washington then ordered Gist from the Eastern Shore and Smallwood from the Western Shore to attack the enemy's rear, allowing Washington to regroup. Fearing that the Marylanders might be cut off from his army, Washington directed them to join him as soon as possible. Gist and Smallwood formed their militias together and hurried to fall in with Brigadier General Anthony Wayne's division in nearby Pennsylvania.

At Paoli, Wayne anticipated being reinforced by the militias of Smallwood and Gist, now only ten miles away. The combined forces would number over four thousand men, certainly a threat to Howe's army. On September 20, Wayne had warnings from locals that a British force would envelop his hilltop camp at Paoli, and he reacted by sending an officer to Smallwood to guide the Maryland militia toward his camp. But before they arrived, Wayne was surprised by the British and suffered heavy casualties. The Maryland militia finally came into action but only confronted the British briefly, as nine militiamen were killed before those remaining fled. So many Maryland militiamen ran that the number of recorded deserters from the force reached almost half of the Maryland army. Gist managed to reform his troops and covered the rear of the retreating Maryland militia. In this exposed position, Gist was ambushed and narrowly escaped injury.

Smallwood and Gist gained their reputations for success as commanders of Continentals rather than militia. Along with their fellow Continental officers, they shared a negative view of the ability of militia. Certainly, the Maryland militia they led to Pennsylvania confirmed that opinion.

CONTINENTAL ARMY

The constant recruitment of the Eastern Shore's best men for the Continental army reduced the area's militia pool and thus its defensive capabilities. By the spring of 1778, with Philadelphia occupied by the British, Loyalism was so strong on the Eastern Shore that the Maryland Board of War ordered army levies to remain there for local defense. The exception was when replacements were needed for Maryland's Continental regiments, and when recruiting took place in March on the Eastern Shore, a surprising 1,057 joined. Of these, the highest number, 158, came from Dorchester County, while Kent was at the lower end, providing only 128, perhaps because its population was the smallest of the counties.

A Continental army had been formed on June 14, 1775, by the Second Continental Congress for the purpose of common defense, adopting the forces outside of Boston and New York. The first ten companies of Continental troops were enlisted for one year, among them riflemen from Pennsylvania, Maryland, Delaware and Virginia, which in 1776 became the First Continental Regiment.

Congress was at pains to counteract the danger of re-creating a force like Oliver Cromwell's New Model Army, which in seventeenth-century England had fostered a military dictatorship. For Continentals, the minimum enlistment age was sixteen, or fifteen with parental consent. Congress felt that the possible youthfulness of recruits could be counteracted by providing for their spiritual welfare, enforcing penalties for failing to attend divine service. Here Congress may have been impressed with the courage of the New Model Army, which had been more spiritually animated than the Continental army would ever be. More effective was the watering down of the use of the court-martial and severe penalties, allowing officers considerable leeway in punishing their men. Such conditions aimed to produce the type of righteous soldiers that a republic could depend on.

Congress did not provide for an army on a long-term basis, and thus it was not as strong as it might have been. This is perfectly understandable, for in 1775, reconciliation was still the watchword, and no one knew the war would continue for eight years. Even though the longest enlistments covered only a year, it was still difficult to recruit for such an extensive time. Recruiting for the Continental army was also a contest with the states, which were the first to offer bounties, a practice that Congress did not adopt until 1777, when it also put the individual states in charge of recruiting Continentals.

OLD LINE CONTINENTALS

Continental units gave Maryland the nickname "Old Line State." The Maryland Line of Continentals achieved a reputation as the saviors of Washington's command. In January 1776, seven

A solider in the Fourth Maryland Independent Company, 1776. One of five Eastern Shore companies created by the convention in January 1776, the Fourth Maryland Independents were initially ordered to Talbot County but by late July had become part the Continental army defending New York. The Seventh Company from Kent County had a similar record. *Company of Military Historians (1981).*

companies of state troops came from the Eastern Shore, one of which, the Seventh Company, contained recruits from Queen Anne's and Kent Counties. Evidently, all the officers were from Queen Anne's County. We know what the Fourth Company looked like and can assume that the Kent County men wore similar linen hunting shirts. By July, these troops were part of Maryland's contribution to the Continental army.

The Maryland Continentals were reorganized in December 1777, continuing their enlistments "for three years or during the war." However, by the close of 1777, few remained from the original line that served at Long Island. Bled weak by fighting in the vanguard of the army, they had only received reinforcements from the Maryland companies of the disbanded Flying Camp. Their pay, usually the responsibility of their state, was often months behind, and yet they were the most trusted units. In later years, the Maryland Continentals went on to serve in the Southern Campaign and were especially commended for their bravery at Guildford Courthouse. Kent County recruits contributed to this glowing reputation.

KENT COUNTY'S MILITARY LEADERSHIP

Authorities like Washington thought that Maryland lacked the officers needed to command its militia and Continentals. While many leaders of Kent County held the honorable title of colonel before the war, these positions were not awarded for military experience but rather in recognition that they were men of standing in the community. They tended to be men of wealth who felt that their constituents owed them deference. When the war began, many signed up to be officers, but the danger of combat, the drudgery and possibility of disease in camp life and the lack of respect shown them discouraged their reenlistment. Only those who were willing to spend years in military service became members of the Continental army. Moreover, such officers were prideful, and they often felt they were victims of discrimination within the army. Personalities clashed among the officers. An activist, Gist was restless for combat with his men, while Smallwood, more of an administrator, seemed unmoved by the sacrifice of his men in battle. For these reasons, most gentleman planters did not serve as officers for long.

JOHN CADWALADER

In a class by himself in Kent County, John Cadwalader was the perfect gentleman planter and an officer with an estimable reputation. Like James Chalmers, Cadwalader, of Pennsylvania, was a newcomer to Kent County, but he was immediately embraced by the county grandees. After all, in 1768, he had married Betsey, the daughter of Edward Lloyd III, one of the Eastern Shore's wealthiest planters, and then squandered much of her money in building one of Philadelphia's most elegant town houses. In Philadelphia, he had persuaded others to protest Parliament's disruption of colonial liberties, and he also knew Thomas Paine. He became a member of Philadelphia's Committee of Safety and captain of a special volunteer City Troop or "Silk Stocking Company." From there, he joined the Continental army, where he served under Washington in the defense of Philadelphia in 1777 as a volunteer.

As the war continued, Cadwalader had found his conservative social and political beliefs in conflict with the supporters of the new Pennsylvania constitution. He defended the right of property and attempted to protect the property of friends like Joseph Galloway, who was a Loyalist. By April 1777, he refused the position of brigadier general of Pennsylvania militia, for he belonged to the party hostile to the new constitution and efforts to implement it. Earlier, he had also refused the position of brigadier general in the Continental army. Although for different reasons, like his friends in Kent County, he felt that his state constitution was flawed.

Early in 1778, Cadwalader explained to George Washington his unfortunate experience with Philadelphia crowds and the radical Pennsylvania constitution that had led him to move to Kent County: "I should have esteemed it an honor to have been continued in the command I had in Pennsylvania, if the government had been such a one as promised that freedom and happiness for which we are contending with Great Britain. I now no longer look upon myself as a resident of that state, and am at a loss to know what part I shall act in this."

When Betsey Lloyd married Cadwalader, her dowry included Shrewsbury Farm on Turner's Creek, Shrewsbury Neck. As his Pennsylvania commercial ventures soured, Cadwalader would spend more time in the rural pleasures of this farm. He could visit seasonally, and he had an overseer, William Gough. To complete a house in 1772 and improve its outbuildings, he began purchasing building materials from John Vorhees of Georgetown and bricks from Turner Creek developer Donaldson Yeates. Cadwalader employed plasterers, masons and painters. As early as June 1774, he was named to the Kent County Committee of Correspondence, even though his principal residence was still in Philadelphia. By 1778, his main home was in Kent County. A year later, after Betsey died, he married Williamina Bond of Philadelphia, who returned with him to Kent County. Cadwalader soon had six hundred arable acres. He continued to purchase land until 1784 and may have planned a more elegant house.

After settling in Kent County, Cadwalader never again served in combat, but he did help to raise militia on the Eastern Shore. As the British occupied Philadelphia in March 1778, he was guardedly optimistic about Eastern Shore militia and supply, explaining, "My fears about provisions and forage, I confess, still give me great pain. Recruiting in [Kent] and [Queen Anne's] county below succeeds better than I expected. One half of the quota required of each county is, I am well informed, made up, and the remainder will soon be completed. The farmers are in great fear of a law to draft the militia; and they are exerting themselves to the utmost in assisting the recruiting officers." Perhaps the new relationship between farmers and recruiters was making a difference that Smallwood and Gist had not experienced. Cadwalader did represent Kent County twice in the Maryland Assembly. In several ways, his perspective would classify him as a grandee, although he was a newcomer.

BREADBASKET ALTERNATIVE

One way of getting beyond the question of the quality of Kent County's militia is to recognize the Eastern Shore's role as a breadbasket. The Delmarva Peninsula has been dubbed the "breadbasket of the Revolution." In 1774, the peninsula supplied as much as one-fifth of the wheat and flour and half of the corn received in Philadelphia. Kent Country produced more wheat than any other county on the peninsula. Arms were included in the supply, as Elisha Winters of Chestertown turned out and repaired muskets and fashioned bayonets for the Maryland Council. Kent County farmers like William Rasin, Robert Read and Abraham Falconer were contractors for barrels, horses and wagons. As a member of the Committee of Observation, Thomas Smyth, the leading grandee, became involved in contracts with locals to supply the militia.

Ideal for the task of raising supplies were men from farming backgrounds, their wealth made in gathering crops, tasks that grandees

Site of Donaldson Yates's commissary, circa 1776–81. Here, where Turners Creek meets the Sassafras River, Yates, eventually deputy quartermaster general of Maryland and Delaware, established a supply depot for the Continental army. Today, this nineteenth-century granary survives on the site of the commissary.

gave to their overseers. As noted, in 1778, the commanders of the two Kent County militia battalions were Colonels Richard Graves of the Thirteenth and Donaldson Yeates of the Twenty-seventh. Merchant Donaldson Yeates had a substantial farm and wharf on Turner's Creek, which fed into the Sassafras River. While he was a militia colonel, he was best at supplying provisions for the Continental army. Early in the war, he was a state contractor, providing beef and pork for the military. In 1777, he was also politically active, severing as a Kent County representative to the Maryland Assembly. By 1780, he became deputy quartermaster general of Maryland and Delaware, the second-highest position at the Continental Depot at Head of Elk. He also continued to gather supplies in Kent County to be sent to Head of Elk.

COMMISSIONERS OF SUPPLY

Late in the war, on April 8, 1780, John Page, Isaac Perkins and Josiah Johnson were named commissioners of supply for Kent County and given the authority to pay for obtaining provisions. Perkins was an officer who is already known to us. Less than a month before this, John Page had been named sheriff of Kent County. In 1777–78, he was also major of the Thirteenth Battalion of Kent County militia, where he served with Major Richard Graves. Page, a planter, owned the lot where one of first public warehouses on Chestertown's waterfront was erected. He was not interested in living in Chestertown, and in the early 1770s, he purchased land at Page's Point on the Chesapeake. Soon after, he built a house at the point, the façades being in Flemish bond, with a kitchen wing located off the south gable. Page had several other properties, as well as a warehouse; thus, his circumstances were ideal for a position in military supply.

We know much less about Josiah Johnson. He was involved in Chester Parish at the end of the war; thus, unlike the others, he may have lived in the Chestertown area. In July 1776, he was an ensign in two companies of Chestertown volunteers destined for the Flying Camp. After the war, he would join Perkins in representing Kent County in the Maryland Assembly.

A Continental commissary was developed at Head of Elk in Cecil County to collect wheat, cattle and other supplies for distribution to the Continental army. From this depot, the Continental army made heavy demands on Eastern Shore farmers not just for food but also for ships, boats and wagons to transport men and supplies. From there, wagons transported the supplies to Delaware's Christiania Bridge. Then, most of the supplies were shipped by water to Wilmington, although some went by wagon to New Castle. Once the supplies reached the Delaware River, they were sent to Philadelphia and then places farther north on the river. In April 1778, the Maryland Council ordered Kent County to send two companies of militia under William Bordley to guard the stores at Head of Elk.

In 1781, the resources of the Eastern Shore were again called upon, this time to prevent the British takeover of Virginia. Orders for the purchase or seizure of 3,100 head of cattle were sent to the county commissaries. The requisition required 1,200 from Worcester and Somerset, 400 from Dorchester, 350 each from Talbot and Queen Anne's, 300 from Kent and 150 from Caroline. Colonel Ephraim Blake, commissar general of the Continental army, went to the Eastern Shore and set up convenient receiving stations at Snow Hill for Worcester and Somerset; Vienna for Dorchester;

Oxford for Talbot, Caroline and Queen Anne's; and Head of Elk for Kent and Cecil. How well this was done is hard to gauge.

Unfortunately, the commissary at Head of Elk was not always able to meet its challenges. When Washington's army arrived there from New York in August 1781 on secret journey to confront Cornwallis at Yorktown, he asked the Maryland legislature for enough vessels to carry his modest 7,500 Franco-American troops to Virginia. The state council responded that "since the enemy has had possession of the bay, our number of sea vessels and craft have been so reduced by captures that we are apprehensive that what remains will not transport so considerable a detachment." Washington had to split his forces between ships that could carry the artillery and fewer than 2,500 men to Annapolis Harbor and the bulk of his force, including the horses of the French cavalry, which marched overland. The chief obstacle to the marchers was crossing the wide Susquehanna River, which they did, later joining the waterborne force. Thus, in September 1781, Washington was finally on his way to Virginia.

Naval Alternative

Some of Chestertown's families made a contribution to the war effort by achieving a measure of naval success. Chestertown played only a minor role in naval protection of Chesapeake Bay because the possibilities of using its waterfront facilities for the Maryland Navy were limited. Nearby Head of Elk outstripped it as a naval station so that Chestertown's wheat and produce were quickly shipped there. In 1777, provisions were also gathered at Charleston in Cecil County and in Princess Anne's County, leaving Chestertown no special claim as center of supply. True, ships were outfitted in Chestertown, but on the whole, the town did not become an arsenal of supply for the Maryland navy.

The naval problem on Chesapeake Bay was that ships sent out and returning risked seizure by British vessels in the bay and along the Atlantic coast. Thus, merchants and militia commissaries supported the formation of the Continental navy and Maryland state navy to protect the coast from the Royal Navy and British privateers based in New York and Nova Scotia. This objective also meant that the Maryland government would raise companies of marines for defense of its Chesapeake and Atlantic coasts. They wore blue hunting shirts and were capable of service afloat or ashore.

To understand the naval situation in Chesapeake Bay, one must review the establishment of Congress's navy from 1775 to 1776. Coverage of Congress's and the state navies during the Revolution tends to focus on privateering, in which individual captains and crews were given letters of marquee and fought merchant vessels in order to obtain prizes and booty. The privateer war combined "freedom and fortune"—goals usually associated with pirates. This attitude may fit in with Hollywood-style swashbuckling, but it has nothing to with what Congress wanted in a navy. In fact, only the states could offer the precious letters of marquee, and Maryland did license 280 privateers during the war.

Most of Congress's ships were converted merchantmen that had been ordered to protect shipping rather than engage in privateering. The captains had difficulties in recruiting sailors because privateers offered higher wages and more opportunities for booty; thus, Congress's ships were often stranded without crews. Regardless of their orders, Congress's captains sought to avoid even the smallest Royal Navy vessel, judging it prudent not to confront it. As the war progressed, naval commanders were inclined to ignore their orders and sail to the possibly richer pickings of merchant ships in Europe and the West Indies. Such an attitude, however, made it difficult for the fledgling navies to protect the Chesapeake coast from British naval depredations.

KENT COUNTY'S CONTINENTAL SHIP CAPTAINS

In Chestertown, three members of the Nicholson family—James, Samuel and John—would serve in the emerging Continental navy, from which they profited. The Nicholsons were not gentlemen planters, for they did not hold land beyond Chestertown; rather, they and their ships were hired by planters for the English trade. The patriarch was Joseph Nicholson, a colonel of Kent County militia and a member of the first Committee of Correspondence in 1774. You will remember that he was involved in the development of Chestertown from the 1730s on and that he and his wife quietly ran the White Swan Tavern, no doubt a hangout for sailors. One of his sons, Joseph Jr., was an attorney, and he served with his father on the Committee of Correspondence in 1774.

Born in 1737, James had the advantage of serving as a junior officer in the Royal Navy and had participated in the Siege of Havana in 1763. Earlier, he been accused and pardoned of killing a sailor in Chestertown. It was his

Joseph Nicholson's White Swan Tavern, circa 1733. Joseph, the father of three Continental navy captains, built this structure and ran the tavern with his wife, Mary.

cargo that caused the Tea Resolves of 1774, but he also served with his father and brother Joseph on the resulting Committee of Correspondence and supported the sending of flour to help the suffering poor of Boston. From October 1776 until 1785, he would be an administrator of the Maryland navy, and Congress named him the senior captain of its navy. However, when the British blocked his fleet in Baltimore Harbor in October 1776, he was forced to abandon his ships and march his men overland to serve with Washington in New York. Despite this, he was made commander of the Maryland navy in 1777 and was given command of the first ship outfitted, the *Defense*.

James was ordered to watch the movements of British and Loyalist ships and escort rebel merchantmen in Chesapeake Bay, a duty that both Congress and the state navy rated as foremost. In the spring of 1778, when

The USS *Trumbull* as depicted on the 1780 gravestone of Jabez Smith in Granary Burying Ground, Boston. James Nicholson served twice as the *Trumbull*'s captain. *Wikimedia Commons.*

the Maryland Assembly built the Continental ship *Virginia*, James was given command. On March 21, the *Virginia* ran aground on Middle Shoal, between the capes, and was easily captured by the British. Nicholson was then twice captain of the *Trumbull*, the last of the original thirteen frigates commissioned by Congress. In 1780, the *Trumbull* engaged the British privateer *Watt* in a fierce duel in which both ships drew off barely seaworthy. A year later, with the newly outfitted *Trumbull*, Nicholson's crew refused to fight, and the ship was taken by a British frigate. In 1781, Nicholson blocked John Paul Jones's lobbying with Congress to become commander of the U.S. Navy because of Jones's lack of seniority and the fact that his naval exploits were as an adjunct to the French navy. James Nicholson was not a great sailor, but he did respect and obey the orders of his superiors.

By 1772, twenty-nine-year-old Samuel was a merchant and owned his own ship, *Molly and Betsy*. When the war broke out in 1775, he was unemployed in London, and he spent the next two years looking for work in Europe before entering the Continental navy as a last resort. He served as a lieutenant on John Paul Jones's *Bon Homme Richard*, operating out of France. While he was given ships in France and at one time cooperated with Lambert Wickes, he was one of a few naval officers who returned to protect the Chesapeake in 1780.

Born in 1756, John served on several vessels and was ultimately captain of the Continental sloop *Hornet*. After the war, John was able to build a brick house on Chestertown's Queen Street in the latest Federalist style.

Another captain, from the old Wickes family, Lambert Wickes was born in 1735 at the family home on Eastern Neck Island near Shipyard Creek. Before the war, Wickes was the captain of the for-hire merchant ships the *Neptune* and the *Ceres*, establishing merchant connections in Philadelphia. In May 1776, Wickes was made captain of the *Reprisal*, in which Congress ordered him to sail against the British frigate *Roebuck*, which was opening the Delaware River to British ships. He evidently failed to do this, as the *Roebuck* took a significant part in Howe's invasion of Chesapeake Bay and the capture of Philadelphia. Wickes was then ordered by Congress to transport William Bingham to a post on Martinique in the West Indies, where he would act as agent for the colonies. In returning, Wickes was to bring munitions for the Continental army.

The *Reprisal* sailed from Philadelphia in June 1776. On the Delaware River, it went to the aid of the harried Continental six-gun brig *Nancy*, which was returning from the West Indies with 386 barrels of gunpowder. The *Nancy* was being chased by six British ships, and to salvage the cargo, its captain ran it aground. Joined by the *Lexington*, the *Reprisal* succeeded in landing almost 200 barrels of powder at Turtle Gut Inlet before the British ships could close the distance. Wickes's brother Richard, his third lieutenant, was killed in the fighting. Clearing the Delaware Capes on July 3, the *Reprisal* continued its voyage, delivering Bingham to Martinique after a sharp engagement with the HMS *Shark*, in which Wickes escaped into port. While in the West Indies, Wickes captured a number of prizes. Certainly, Wickes did not return to guard duty in the Delaware Capes. In fact, he would never return to the United States.

The rest of Wickes's career in France, the English Channel, Biscay Bay and Ireland, where he raided English merchantmen from the safety of French ports, is beyond our scope. He finally left Europe for home in October 1777, but *Reprisal* foundered off the Grand Banks of Newfoundland, with the loss of all hands except the cook. Wickes's short and flamboyant career as a Continental captain was over.

Bread, not militia or naval exploits, was Kent County's key contribution to the rebel military. Because Kent County's military leadership was best at supply, it did not produce any notable soldiers, with the exception of those in Maryland's Continental regiments. The new middling leadership came from wealthy farmers and millers such as Perkins and Yeates and was based in the countryside rather than in Chestertown. The production of foodstuffs, arms and ships was best served in the countryside. The grandees' early support of the rebel cause declined, perhaps reflecting their aging but also their disagreement with the policies of the state government in Annapolis.

Overall, the militia system in Kent County did not work well. Recruiting seems to have produced unarmed, unclothed, untrained and leaderless men, who reached their nadir in 1777, when the militias of Smallwood and Gist were routed in Pennsylvania. The militia also bore the brunt of the continuing Eastern Shore Loyalist insurrection so that time to recuperate never existed. The Continental and Maryland navies were unable to fulfill the goal of protecting rebel shipping in Chesapeake Bay, and for much of the war, the Royal Navy and Loyalist privateers closed the bay to rebel trade. Here we see the reality of fighting a war that prosperous Kent County was neither psychologically prepared for nor completely committed to.

Chapter 8
Loyalism in the Making

During the war, the Eastern Shore was divided not only by social and religious conflict but also by rebels and Loyalists. Loyalism was forced into the open because rebel authorities would not allow the existence of a loyal opposition. If you were not for them, you were automatically against them. Members of the existing political elite tended to make reluctant revolutionaries who feared anarchy more than Parliament's taxes. It is possible that a growing neutral position was the most accepted by the Eastern Shore's leadership.

Disaffection on the Eastern Shore had begun in 1775 as a reaction against the newly formed conventions and constitutional government in Annapolis. Loyalty to the king and Governor Eden were mixed with hostility to the conservative grandees, who perpetuated their rule by restricting those who could vote and hold office. Loyalism was promoted when Governor Eden realized the militia was in the hands of the new government, leaving him without military power. By the end of 1775, he formed a Protective Association, a paramilitary group that had 1,900 members capable of bearing arms. The association was created in the tradition of English law as a *posse comitatus*, coming together when its members were threatened. It was supported by "moderate people under the necessity of uniting for our own defense after being threatened with expulsion [and] loss of life for not acceding to what we deem treason and rebellion."

The Protective Association was popular on the Eastern Shore. The hostility to new government was so imbedded in its society that this was only the beginning of an attitude that would last throughout the entire war. In November 1775, before the Worcester County Court, Isaac Hammond admitted that he and forty others had attended a meeting to form an association that agreed to stand together on behalf of the king to oppose the Worcester County Committee of Observation. They were to support one another within twenty-four hours' warning and thus rescue their fellow members. A week later, Barclay White claimed that it was not only protection that concerned them but also "to frustrate the [new] government's control of the region." He warned that the associates intended to "take the Worcester County Committee out of their beds in the dead of night" and take them to Lord Dunmore. In adjacent Somerset County, a rebel reported to the Annapolis-based Committee of Safety that "an association under the most solemn oath of secrecy and entirely repugnant to the resolves of the...[Maryland] Convention has been subscribed by more than one hundred inhabitants of these counties...who are ready to receive the yoke of bondage from the hands of the British Parliament." However, these associations do not seem to have endured beyond the early years of the war.

Many were Loyalists because they did not believe that independence was necessary. As early as June 1775, Isaac Costen organized two hundred men in Somerset County to oppose the movement for independence. As a result, he was declared "inimical to the cause of American freedom" and sentenced to jail. But his supporters soon obtained his release. Too many people were "disaffected" for the Annapolis government to react. In 1778, Costen led Loyalist raiders to the home of militia captain John Williams. Costen then went to Philadelphia to join Chalmers's Loyalist regiment.

As shown, the rebels formed their own association in the summer of 1775 at Annapolis and ordered the county Committees of Observation to round up signatories and note who avoided the signing, defining them as non-associators. At the time, no effort was made to persecute the non-associators, but by January 1776, the convention required that they receive parole for their good conduct, that their arms be confiscated, that higher taxes be levied on them and that the local committees watch them. In 1780, John Chalmers would claim that the non-associators in Maryland numbered twelve thousand, but he was bound to overestimate. Records of examining committees in the courts show that the non-associators felt that the rebels were acting not for the defense of liberty or property "but for the purpose of enslaving the poor people thereof." Moreover, even if they were forced to sign a paper, it did not alter the true feelings of the disaffected.

LORD DUNMORE IN THE BACKGROUND

In addition to Eden's association, in 1775, Lord Dunmore, the royal governor of Virginia, had a direct effect upon the development of Loyalism in Chesapeake Bay. He had been forced to flee the capital of Williamsburg for the safety of the port town of Norfolk, where he formed a fleet, which included the HMS *Fowley*, to cruise the Chesapeake. His loyal forces had been reduced to only three hundred men. To raise troops, Dunmore issued a proclamation calling on all able-bodied men to assist him in the defense of the colony, including the slaves of rebels, who were promised their freedom in exchange for service in his army. This was so controversial that some thought Dunmore had gone mad, especially Loyalist slaveholders, who feared a slave rebellion as much as anybody. Still, this strategy was successful in attracting black recruits. Within a month, Dunmore had raised eight hundred soldiers, mostly blacks, to form the Ethiopian Regiment. Dunmore's proclamation became the basis of the first mass emancipation of slaves in colonial history.

A 1907 American Color Type postcard of James Murray, fourth Earl of Dunmore and governor of Virginia, greeting the twenty-four-gun HMS *Fowey*. Murray's proclamation offered freedom to slaves, who joined him as he moved about the Chesapeake spreading fear of slave rebellion among the planter families. *Library of Congress.*

The Virginia Congress replied immediately to Dunmore's proclamation by branding his offer of freedom as a strike at the foundations of Virginia's plantation society. It proceeded to threaten the death penalty to escaping slaves. Certainly, the slaveholding grandees of Virginia found Dunmore's proclamation to be an impetus to abandon the royal government and support independence.

When the Declaration of Independence was written, it was rumored that Lord Dunmore's fleet would attempt to occupy the Eastern Shore. As Dunmore was nearby, from Dorchester County came a dispatch implying that whites were working with blacks to induce them to support the king's cause. Dunmore's forces were ultimately decimated by a smallpox outbreak and defeated. When Dunmore left Chesapeake Bay in 1776, he took three hundred former slaves with him to New York.

It was against the background of Dunmore's amphibious presence that slave insurrections were feared on the Eastern Shore. Evidently, Dunmore had supporters there. It was noted that "the insolence of the Negros in this county is come to such a height that we are under the necessity of disarming them, which we affected on Saturday last. We took about eighty guns, some bayonets, swords, etc." Independence was supported by slaveholders, many of whom feared what might happen in a slave uprising.

SLAVES AND POOR WHITES

Certainly the development of Loyalism on the Eastern Shore was affected by the issue of slavery. Slaves were becoming Loyalists by threatening the plantation economy of wealthy rebels. In 1775, the Eastern Shore's free blacks and slaves had already become restless, posing a threat to the stability of the plantation economy. Maryland's June convention admitted that an insurrection of slaves was feared, chiefly in coordination with Lord Dunmore. On July 22, Maryland governor Thomas Johnson observed that Eastern Shore planters "reluctantly leave their own neighborhoods unhappily full of Negros who might, it is likely, on any misfortune to our militia become very dangerous." In August, three Dorchester County slaves who had killed a white man in an unsuccessful bid for freedom were executed in typical fashion by having their right hands cut off and then being hanged. The Dorchester County court system was put to use when a grand jury was summoned to investigate the evidence of insurrectionist plots, especially those involving whites and blacks.

While the bulk of these insurgents were from the lower orders, their leadership often came from the middling sort. A wheelwright and Loyalist, John Simmons saw blacks and whites as working together against exploitation by gentlemen planters. He proposed that if he could get a few more whites to support him, he would get "all the Negros in the Dorchester County" to rebel against their wealthy masters. If they could get ammunition, they would kill all the gentlemen and "have the best of the land to tend." It was reported that men calling for a militia muster were, in fact, organizing to overthrow "the gentlemen [who] were intending to fight for their lands and Negros." Wealthy and distressed Eastern Shore gentry sent their families and dependents across the bay to safety.

When slaves were encouraged to join Lord Dunmore, one rebel planter claimed, "The malicious and impudent speeches of some among the lower classes of whites have induced them to believe that their freedom depends upon the success of the King's troops. We cannot therefore be too vigilant nor too rigorous with those who promote and encourage this disposition in our slaves." The alliance of the lower orders, operating to further their interests, angered the aristocratic gentlemen planters. Late in August 1777, an official reported from Cecil County that he lacked soldiers "to prevent the Negros, servants and disaffected people from going over to the enemy." He admitted that already "several Negros are gone from our parts on board [British ships], and some white people." Situations like these showed that blacks and poor whites were uniting because of their frustration with their position at the bottom of society.

THE ROYAL NAVY

The Royal Navy constantly occupied Chesapeake Bay during the war and was regarded by rebel authorities as one of the chief instigators of Loyalism. In the colonies, it was a momentous task for the Royal Navy to patrol the long coastline, which on account of trade connections stretched all the way to the West Indies. The Royal Navy also had the duty of protecting Atlantic convoys of troops and supplies. It could also involve itself in local affairs, as in February 1777, when Loyalists collected 250 men near Salisbury in Somerset County along with "three field pieces, which they received from the HMS *Roebuck* with some seamen, with the intention to seize the magazine and destroy the property of the [rebels]. Normally there would be three men-of-war in the bay, one at Tangiers, one at Smith's Point and one in the middle."

When Sir William Howe invaded Chesapeake Bay in August 1777, his fleet moved toward Chestertown and then to Head of Elk. By August 21, the fleet was off the Patapsco River near Baltimore. The following day, it

A mezzotint of Lieutenant General Howe, London, 1777. A brilliant tactician, Howe was slow to take advantage of his many victories, for he harbored hopes of reconciliation that soon led him to create Loyalist military units. *Author's collection.*

crossed the bay to Swan Point and, the day after, moored off the Sassafras River, where a pilot came aboard the HMS *Somerset*. Howe sent a party of seamen and officers, which supposedly included James Chalmers, to Chestertown to meet Loyalists. On August 24, the majority of the fleet proceeded to Turkey Point, with some ships remaining off the Sassafras. A white man and three blacks came off, and a long boat and pinnace went ashore. The men wanted to exchange fresh provisions, rather than money, for salt from the ships. In fact, the only commodity aside from arms and ammunition carried by the Royal Navy was salt, something that, as we have seen, the people on the Eastern Shore were willing to fight for. On the twenty-fifth, the fleet sailed up the Elk River and lay opposite Cecil Court House. British troops then landed on the west side of the Elk River in five disembarkations.

Howe attempted to gain Loyalist support on the Eastern Shore. By this time, he still hoped for reconciliation, but it was now based on strong support of Loyalism, including the establishment and arming of provincial regiments. Following these convictions, in August 1777, near Head of Elk, Howe issued a proclamation to the peaceable inhabitants of Pennsylvania, Delaware and the Eastern Shore. He offered a pardon to residents who had taken up arms against the king if they would voluntarily surrender themselves to the king's troops. It was a tempting offer, especially for the disaffected among the militia being gathered to oppose him. He also offered protection to those "not guilty of having assumed legislative or judicial authority," having "acted illegally in subordinate stations" and having "been induced to leave their dwellings, provided such persons do forthwith return, and remain peaceably at their usual places of abode." Here was a promise of sanctuary to the ordinary supporters of the rebel cause. In terms of the rebel military, Howe offered "a free and general pardon to all officers and privates, as shall voluntarily come and surrender themselves to any detachment of His Majesty's forces." Ships in his fleet distributed the proclamation. This was British pacification at its best, and it offered Kent County's Loyalists a reason for being.

Howe was also aware of the need to restrain his troops, warning that "punishment shall be inflicted upon those [of his troops] who shall dare to plunder the property, or molest the persons of his Majesty's well-disposed subjects." He notably failed in this policy, for in all armies, the temptation to plunder usually overwhelmed discipline.

The Royal Navy would continue to serve in Chesapeake Bay until the end of the war. Late in 1780, Major General Alexander Leslie was sent to Chesapeake Bay to make a diversion that would help Cornwallis's army to the south by striking at the magazines collected by the rebels for supplying an army to oppose him. For the Loyalists of Tidewater Maryland, the presence of Leslie and his naval squadron, commanded by Captain George Gayton, inspired support for Britain. After Gayton's arrival, the bay was covered with Loyalist barges, galleys and privateers that foraged into the rivers of the defenseless Eastern Shore. They not only aimed at taking ships and ports but also hinted at destroying the plantations and country seats of the rebel elite.

KENT COUNTY LOYALIST DEPREDATIONS

Kent County was raided by Loyalists, with the Chesapeake coast serving as the field of action. In September 1777, Mary Gittings reported that her house had been plundered by Loyalists, who took her furniture, clothing and household items. When she petitioned for redress of her tax obligation to the Kent County Collection of Assessment, she was informed that she would not have to pay taxes for the year 1779. That year, Congress received word that British officers were gathering a band of Loyalists at the head of the Chester River.

In 1781, communications between the Eastern and Western Shores were completely disrupted. Loyalists were prevented from penetrating the Kent County coast by a troop of Kent County horsemen. After a destructive March raid by the British along the Wye River, William Bordley, whose property had been destroyed, brought Kent County militia to the Wye and stationed them at strategic points to oppose four hostile sloops and schooners that had been lingering off shore.

It has been shown that the chief incident of Loyalist insurrection came in June 1780, when Perkins's mills were burned down at night by supposed Kent County Loyalists. Colonel Perkins reported that "my invaluable set of mills were burned to the ground on the 27th instant at night before I reached home from Annapolis, my conjectures are that [Loyalists] in the upper part of this county [were responsible]."

While its motives were religious rather than political, it must be remembered that many saw Methodism as Loyalism. It has been seen that in June 1778, itinerant Freeborn Garrettson's Methodism nearly cost him his life. This act of violence, which took place on the way to Chestertown, was duplicated in Caroline, Talbot and Dorchester Counties, immediately to the south of Kent. The heated crowd may have been approved of by some Anglican vestry as a means of obstructing evangelism, which they saw as an anarchist undermining of their authority.

Anglican Churchmen

Loyalism did not appear solely in the form of insurrection or the Royal Navy; it was also a matter of winning men's minds. Regardless of the Garrettson incident, many Anglicans were consistently Loyalists. In explaining the disaffection of Loyalists on the Eastern Shore in March 1777, General Smallwood claimed that religion was "the original cause" of the alienation from the rebel cause and that the greatest number "conceal their true motives and make religion a cloak for their nefarious designs." He felt Anglican churches were being used to hide Loyalists.

It is known that in 1775, all three of Kent County's parish parsons—John Patterson, Robert Read and John Montgomery—elected to say prayers for the king and lost their positions. Read chose to go quietly to Virginia, but Montgomery was more outspoken. Although he was invited to be Shrewsbury's parson, he soon left for London, returning to New York City in 1777, where he supported Loyalism. Chester Parish had an even more active Loyalist parson, John Patterson. Between 1766 and 1775, that parish had three unassuming rectors responsible for the church at Worton and chapel at Chestertown. Patterson succeeded in 1775, but his views soon made him the last rector of the established Anglican Church. No Chester Parish vestry met between 1774 and 1779, so it was left to Patterson to conduct parish matters.

On August 21, 1775, Patterson's refusal to give up prayers for the king landed him before the Kent County Committee of Observation. He offended them blatantly, as he felt that there was "more liberty in Turkey than in this province." He affiliated himself with Reverend Jonathan Boucher of Annapolis, who worked against the rebellion. When Howe's fleet anchored at the Sassafras River in September 1777, Chalmers landed in Chestertown and took refuge in Patterson's house. Here, Chalmers gained intelligence from Patterson and William Slubey and then rejoined the fleet. Soon after Chalmers's visit, Patterson was seized by the committee and taken across the bay to be confined in Baltimore County.

The grandee William Paca then had Patterson sent as a prisoner to Virginia. Paca assessed that Patterson "has been endeavoring to throw every obstacle in the way of calling forth our militia…and has violated the execution of our laws. He is the most provoking exasperating mortal that ever existed. We have great reasons to suspect him of being concerned with one [James Chalmers] of [Kent] County, who now is with the enemy conducting them on their ravaging and plundering parties." Patterson was finally released in March 1778 on the condition that he would mind his tongue. He traveled immediately to British-occupied Philadelphia, where he was named chaplain of Chalmers's regiment.

JAMES CHALMERS

Kent County's leading Loyalist was planter and author James Chalmers. Born in Elgin, Moray, Scotland, in 1732, Chalmers came to Kent County in 1760 with several slaves and much wealth. After developing a wheat plantation on a seven-mile-long, well-cultivated island, he bought more land in other areas around Chestertown, as well as two lots within the town, totaling 584 acres. In 1769, he entertained Governor Robert Eden and his party when they visited the Eastern Shore. A year later, he was a pew holder in the Chester Anglican Chapel. He was said to have been respected in Maryland and Delaware as being both well bred and well informed. However, he was not part of Kent County's old family network.

In June 1777, Chalmers went to New York City and offered advice to one of Howe's aids on the weakness of the rebels in New Jersey. In August, at Head of Elk, Chalmers met Howe and explained that he had been busy in completing a unit of Loyalists. He also helped to gather horses in Cecil and Kent Counties for transporting Howe's supplies. Chalmers was with Howe's victorious army at Brandywine. In Philadelphia on October 14, 1777, Howe commissioned Chalmers lieutenant colonel of the First Battalion of Maryland Loyalists, which was authorized at a strength of four hundred privates.

This followed Howe's policy of creating Loyalist regiments to strengthen support for the British cause as opposed to simply fulfilling a need for manpower. The unit would help to quell the "unnatural rebellion" and protect Maryland. It would "receive the same pay and be under the same discipline as His Majesty's regular troops." To help with recruiting, a bounty of five dollars was authorized. For the moment, the regiment was to be directly under Howe's orders. Ten days later, Howe approved of a list of nine

A private in the Maryland Loyalist Regiment, recruited throughout Maryland by James Chalmers, circa 1779–81. Sir William Howe saw to it that the unit was part of the provincial establishment. It fought in many places but never in Maryland. *Company of Military Historians (1981).*

officers for the regiment. These officers were to raise the men for the unit, but as might be expected, only two on the list, Walter Dulany and Adam Allen, succeeded in doing this. Others would take their place. Chalmers must have gone back to Chestertown to bring Eastern Shore Loyalists to Philadelphia. By May 1778, the battalion, numbering 336—close to its authorized strength—was ready for action in Philadelphia.

The new battalion left Philadelphia for New York during the evacuation of June 1778. Because it was no mere volunteer band, such as was often found about the Chesepeake, it went with the British army as part of the provincial establishment of Loyalist units. Sir Henry Clinton, having replaced Howe, was now in command of the evacuation, which had been ordered by the ministry in London. The army, with a baggage train and many camp followers, traveled across New Jersey until it reached Sandy Hook on July 4. From there, it was ferried to Staten Island and New York. On the way, at Monmouth Courthouse, Washington's army caught up with Clinton's rear guard, and a battle took place between a portion of Clinton's army, led by Lord Cornwallis, and Washington's force. The Maryland Loyalists were first tested in this fight, in which the evacuation continued successfully, not a single wagon being lost. Upon arrival in New York, Clinton assigned the unit to Long Island, where it participated in foraging and supply operations.

As he waited for action on Long Island in 1779–80, Chalmers wrote a series of plans urging Clinton to send a small expedition to occupy Delmarva. This expedition would cut off supplies to Washington; destroy rebel strongholds like Baltimore and Annapolis; occupy Oxford, Head of Elk and Chestertown; and invade Virginia. Chalmers wanted the invaders to permanently occupy Delmarva. For a moment in April 1781, it looked like the Eastern Shore would again be involved in a British invasion of Delmarva. Intelligence came to Washington that Clinton would leave New York with a force to penetrate the Delaware River and make New Castle the center of his operations, encompassing the Delmarva Peninsula. In New York, Clinton had written of the need to make the Chesapeake and the Delaware, "where the friends of the king were numerous," centers of offensive action. Not until Lord Charles Cornwallis moved his army into Virginia does Clinton seem to have heeded these plans, which required a combination of naval and Loyalist support. But Clinton was diverted, and the expedition seemed less necessary as Cornwallis swept Virginia.

CAPTAIN JAMES FRISBY'S FAMILY

You will remember the Frisbys as an old Chestertown family related to the Ringgolds and Smyths. As leading planters by the 1760s, the Frisbys held two great plantations: Hinchingham and what would become known as Violet Farm. They also had a Chestertown house built around 1766, probably for James Sr., on Front Street. While located among the grandees' houses, the Frisby house was uniquely modest.

The War for Independence divided the Frisbys. James Sr. appears to have retired to his estates, avoiding the conflict. However, his son William was active in the Kent County militia, in 1776 becoming captain of a company and, two years later, a major of the Thirteenth Battalion under William Bordley and Isaac Perkins. Another son, Richard, had no military career but was a member of the Chester Parish vestry in 1767 and, a decade later, a justice of the Kent County Orphans Court. His eldest son, James Frisby Jr., was different. He arrived in Philadelphia in 1777 and met Chalmers, signing up to be the captain of a company in his regiment. James Jr. must have returned to Kent County to raise his company. He would serve in the Maryland Loyalists until the very end of the war, resigning his commission in Canada in the spring of 1783.

THE SLUBEY BROTHERS

Brothers Nicholas and William Slubey, both merchant Loyalists, survived the war and returned to Chestertown to reestablish their businesses as if the war had never happened. Nicholas Slubey knew Chalmers, and he joined the Loyalists in New York after being charged with treason by the state council in 1779. In the spring of 1781, he worked with William to provide intelligence on Delmarva's aggregate figures for wheat, flour and Indian corn produced during the years 1770–75. After the war, he returned home and reestablished himself as a grain merchant. By 1788, with the decline of the European grain market in Chestertown, he moved to Baltimore.

William Slubey, who owned a pew in the Chester Chapel in 1772, met with Chalmers at Reverend Patterson's house to provide intelligence in September 1777. In the summer of 1779, William was identified as a Loyalist by the state council and charged with treason. However, he came back after the war and in 1786 purchased Worrell's Tavern from Edward Worrell, who was deeply in debt to Slubey. Ten years later, he purchased property on Front Street from Thomas Ringgold VI. William stayed in Chestertown and died there in 1803. It is evident that the Slubey brothers did not suffer economically for their Loyalist views.

DIASPORA

After the war, men of the Maryland Loyalist Regiment, as well as other Loyalists from various colonies, were transported to a new homeland in Nova Scotia at the expense of the British government. In the fall of 1783, however, the ship carrying members of the First Battalion of Maryland Loyalists was wrecked off the Maritime Coast. Thus, the survivors became the first citizens of the site of the wreck, the province of New Brunswick. Captain Caleb Jones, who had joined Lord Dunmore's fleet and kept the unit's orderly book, did well in New Brunswick, being one of the original grantees of St. John's and acquiring much land. Captain Philip Barton Key purchased several adjoining lots in New Brunswick from the men in his company. He then went to England to study law at the Middle Temple. In 1785, he returned to Maryland and read law for his admission to the bar. His nephew, Francis Scott Key, eventually studied law under him. When New York was evacuated, James Chambers returned to England and wrote another pamphlet attacking Paine's economic policies and another regarding war in Santo Domingo. He socialized with William Franklin, former governor of New Jersey, and died in 1806 in Chelsea, London.

LOTS OF ROBIN HOODS, BUT NO KING RICHARD

On the Eastern Shore, Loyalism developed piecemeal, and its authority lacked a sense of legitimacy. It was as in medieval England, when Robin Hood appeared as a bandit, robbing from the rich and giving to the poor until he met King Richard and could legitimately serve His Majesty. Such legitimacy did not develop off the Eastern Shore. Governor Eden's Protective Association was fleeting, and the proclamations of Dunmore and Howe were effective only as long as they were present. While the Annapolis state government had a similar lack of legitimacy, its core institutions remained secure because they were based on the other side of the Chesapeake Bay.

Loyalism was enhanced by the mere presence of a Royal Navy ship on the bay. Loyalist activity was supported by elements of the lower sort and led by men of the middling sort. The mere threat of a slave uprising made most gentry avoid Loyalism. Planters like the devoted Chalmers were few; it was ultimately safer for grandees to work around the war, even if they were critical of the new state government's direction. Chalmers and the Maryland Loyalist Regiment never got to serve in Maryland because Sir Henry Clinton needed the regiment in other theaters of the war and never seemed ready to send an army back to Delmarva.

Chestertown and Kent County were not leading centers of Loyalism when compared to the rest of the Eastern Shore. However, it may be that the rivalry between the growing number of Methodists and the Anglican parish vestries was stronger here than elsewhere, thus contributing to both religious and political discord.

Chapter 9
Affirmations

It would be inspiring to say that Chestertown and Kent County were in the forefront of the Revolution's "patriot cause," a place that Mel Gibson's movie *The Patriot* would emulate. But such is not reality. Kent County was spilt not only between Loyalists and rebels but also between Anglicans and Methodists. As for the social orders, the upper, middling and lower sorts were, at times, in opposition to each other. The grandees and gentry were not consistent on where they stood because they tended toward moderation. It is safest to say that these times were far more complicated than is realized and to admit that Kent County and Chestertown were not prominent in the independence movement or the resulting war. The Kent County situation may be the norm, however, much closer to the total picture than what is presented in histories that focus purely on politics in Philadelphia or decisive battles. Make no mistake, though, our story is one of brave men, supportive women and frustrated black slaves dealing with the crucial aspects of everyday life, which collectively made a difference in the outcome of the Revolution on the Eastern Shore.

After the war, Chestertown and Kent County were on their way to becoming part of the Eastern Shore we know today. Actually, time would stand still, as farming would remain the mainstay of the economy even after middling farmers had disappeared in most parts of our country. Thus, the area has a pristine eighteenth-century economy still existing in the twenty-first century. It is rare that such an extensive cultivated landscape exists today, as witnessed by the fact that while Colonial Williamsburg looks like it did in the past, its environs are overwhelmed by modern development.

The Chesapeake and its tributaries continue to provide a backdrop for the great sailing traditions that exist today, especially in reproductions like the *Sultana*. And then there is the delicious bounty of crab, oyster and clam that is presented in feasts dubbed "crab fests." Actually, this is something relatively new. In the eighteenth century, such fare was not prized; it was the chief source of protein for the lower orders and certainly graced only a small corner of a grandee's table. Some things really have changed!

Selected Bibliography

Primary Sources

Andre, John. *Major Andre's Journal*. Tarrytown, NY: William Abbatt, 1930.

Chalmers, James. *Plain Truth: Addressed to the Inhabitants of America*. Dublin, Ireland: M. Mills, 1776.

Dickinson, John. *Letters from a Farmer in Pennsylvania*. Englewood Cliffs, NJ: Prentice Hall, 1962.

Douglass, Frederick. *The Life and Times of Frederick Douglass*. Hertfordshire, UK: Wordsworth Editions Limited, 1996.

Paine, Thomas. *Common Sense*. London: Penguin Classics, 1982.

Peden, Henry, Jr., ed. *Inhabitants of Kent County, Maryland, 1637–1787*. Westminster, MD: Heritage Books, 2007.

———. *Revolutionary Patriots of Kent and Queen Anne's Counties*. Westminster, MD: Willow Bend Books, 2000.

Secondary Sources

Bourne, Michael. *Historic Houses of Kent County: An Architectural History, 1642–1860*. Chestertown, MD: Chester River Press, 2008.

Calderhead, William. "Prelude to Yorktown." *Maryland History Magazine* 77, no. 2 (June 1982): 123–35.

Clemens, Paul. *The Atlantic Economy and Colonial Maryland's Eastern Shore: From Tobacco to Grain*. Ithaca, NY: Cornell University, 1980.

Corbett, Theodore. *Revolutionary New Castle: The Struggle for Independence*. Charleston, SC: The History Press, 2012.

Daniels, Christine. "From Father to Son: Economic Roots of Craft Dynamics in Eighteenth-Century Maryland." In *American Artisans: Crafting Social Identity, 1750–1850*. Edited by Howard B. Rock, Paul A. Gilje and Robert Asher. Baltimore, MD: Johns Hopkins University Press, 1995.

DeProspero, Katherine Myrick. *A History of Shrewsbury Parish Church*. Wye Mills, MD: Chesepeake College Press, 1988.

Dolde, Jenifer Grindle. *Trumpington: A Legacy of Land on the Chesapeake Bay: Three Centuries of Family and Farming in Kent County, Maryland*. N.p.: T.H. Publishing, 2006.

Goodheart, Adam. "Tea and Fantasy: Fact, Fiction, and Revolution in an American Town." *The American Scholar* 74, no. 4 (Autumn 2005).

Hanson, George. *Old Kent: The Eastern Shore of Maryland*. Baltimore, MD: Regional Publishing Company, 1967.

Hoffman, Ronald. *A Spirit of Dissension: Economics, Politics, and the Revolution in Maryland*. Baltimore, MD: Johns Hopkins University Press, 1973.

Kowalewski, Albin. "An Imperfect Institution: Slavery's Legacy at Washington College." The Revolutionary College Project. www.washcoll. edu/centers/starr/revcollege/struggleandstrength/slavery.html.

Leekley, John. Paper for Professor Dugan's class. Georgetown University, Washington, D.C.

Maier, Pauline. *From Resistance to Revolution: Colonial Radicals and the Development of American Opposition to Britain, 1765–1776*. New York: Alfred A. Knopf, 1973.

McCall, Davy. *A Tricentennial History of St. Paul's Church, Kent*. Chestertown, MD: St. Paul's Church, 1993.

Neville, Barry. "For God, King, and Country: Loyalism on the Eastern Shore of Maryland During the American Revolution." *International Social Science Review* 84, no. 3–4 (Fall–Winter 2009).

New, M. Christopher. *Maryland Loyalists in the American Revolution*. Centreville, MD: Tidewater Publishers, 1996.

Norton, Mary Beth. "Gender and Defamation in Seventeenth-Century Maryland." *William and Mary Quarterly* 44, no .1 (January 1987).

Papenfuse, Edward. *In Pursuit of Profit: The Annapolis Merchants in the Era of the American Revolution, 1763–1805*. Baltimore, MD: Johns Hopkins University Press, 1975.

Shomette, Donald. *Pirates on the Chesapeake*. Centreville, MD: Tidewater Publishers, 1985.

S.L. Rogers Design. "Turner Creek & Sassafras NRMA Interpretive Plan." November 2006.

Smith, Digby, and Kevin Kiley. *An Illustrated Encyclopedia of Uniforms of the American War of Independence, 1775–1783*. London: Lorenz Books, 2008.

Truitt, Charles. *Breadbasket of the Revolution: Delmarva's Eight Turbulent War Years*. Baltimore, MD: Publication Press, 1975.

Usilton, Fred. *History of Kent County, Maryland, 1630–1916*. Chestertown, MD: Perry Publications, 1916.

Vivian, Jean. "Thomas Stone and the Reorganization of the Maryland Council of Safety, 1776." *Maryland History Magazine* 69, no. 3 (Fall 1974): 271–78.

Williams, William. *The Garden of American Methodism: The Delmarva Peninsula, 1760–1820*. Wilmington, DE: Scholarly Resources, 1984.

Index

T

Talbot County 17, 33, 34, 64, 93, 97,
    102, 103, 109, 122, 136
tobacco 14, 22, 26, 32, 34, 36, 39, 40,
    41, 42, 45, 52, 56, 59, 61, 62,
    70, 91
Trumbull (frigate) 126

V

vestry 24, 28, 31, 32, 38, 43, 56, 57, 58,
    59, 61, 62, 63, 67, 68, 137, 141
Virginia 27, 29, 31, 32, 36, 41, 60, 63,
    92, 110, 116, 122, 123, 126,
    131, 132, 137, 140

W

Washington, George 13, 48, 92, 110,
    114, 115, 117, 119, 123, 125, 140
Wayne, Anthony 115
West Indies 15, 21, 38, 86, 124, 127, 133
wheat 14, 15, 22, 26, 29, 34, 35, 36,
    43, 51, 52, 53, 62, 70, 86, 91,
    96, 104, 120, 122, 123, 138, 141
White Swan Tavern 38, 124
Wickes, Joseph 26, 27, 29
Wickes, Lambert 127
Wickes, Simon 53, 62
Widehall 50, 104
Worcester County 17, 100, 110, 113,
    114, 122, 130

Y

Yeates, Donaldson 25, 98, 101, 108,
    119, 121

About the Author

A Delaware resident, Ted Corbett has a PhD in history and is an expert on the Revolutionary War era. The thrust of his work is military history, but his specialty is putting local military activity into social, economic, religious and political contexts. His books include *No Turning Point: The Saratoga Campaign in Perspective* (2012), *Pirates and Privateers of St. Augustine* (2012), *Revolutionary New Castle* (2012), *A Home in the Battenkill Valley: The Early Years of Susan B. Anthony* (2007), *A Clash of Cultures on the Warpath of Nations* (2002), *The Making of American Resorts* (2001) and more.